English Readings

이혜경
안필규
이 철
편저

북코리아

English Readings

CONTENTS

What Are We at College for?

Randall Stewart*

A college is a community, and a community consists of people who are bound together by personal ties. The relation between teacher and student is a personal relation. There must be a mutual interest, a mutual helpfulness. No mechanical device can ever take the place of this personal connection. No TV screen can respond to your responses, or share your joys and sorrows, or chat with you over a coke or coffee in the Commodore Room.[1] To mechanize education, to depersonalize it, is to deprive it of its most precious ingredient. Let us cherish this personal ele-

* Randall Stewart : Vanderbilt대학의 영문학 교수. 저서로는 *Nathaniel Hawthorne : A Biography*(1948), *American Literature and Christian Doctrine* 등이 있음.

1) Commodore Room : student lounge

ment at all costs. Vanderbilt, fortunately, is not too big for us to know one another, and take an interest in one another. Vanderbilt is not too big for us to be friends.

A student's life is filled with a number of things.

This time of year, we should all go out and cheer for the team. Some places overemphasize football, but Vanderbilt is not one of those places. We know that a great football team doesn't make a great college. We know that Oklahoma could beat Harvard fifty to nothing[2)] any Saturday, yet Harvard is greater university than Oklahoma. We know all these things, but we still have a perfect right to like football. Our life would lose a lot of color and zest without it.

Activities are good and beneficial, in moderation, but activities alone don't make a college. The student should give serious attention to his studies. He is here to learn, and to think. A good college has an atmosphere of studiousness, and of intellectual inquiry. This is a cooperative effort between students and faculty. The student should read the assignment regularly, in advance of the class meeting and if the class is small enough to permit the free exchange of ideas, the class ought to be conducted, in part at least, on a discussion basis. The student should feel an obligation to contribute something, to pull his weight in the boat. The unprepared student, who comes to class, childlike, with his empty pail, expecting the professor to fill it, without any effort on the student's part; the student who

---

2) fifty to nothing : 50 : 0

has a purely passive attitude; the rote-student who memorizes the class notes, and hands them back on the examination without generating a single idea of his own—that student is not getting an education, and a professor who conducts that kind of a course is not doing the job he ought to do.

Vanderbilt has always stood for the higher literacy, and by the higher literacy I mean the ability to read intelligently and write respectably. Reading intelligently means more than the ability to pronounce the words; it means understanding what is read, understanding the meaning or meanings; reading between the lines, catching the overtones, discovering and uncovering layers of meanings, as in a novel by Faulkner[3)] or a play by Shakespeare. And writing respectably means more than so-called "proficiency," matching verbs and nouns, and the like. It means writing with discrimination,[4)] with a feeling for words. Words are wonderful instruments, but very tricky, and one has to know what he is about when he uses them. In our Freshman English course, we have both reading and writing. They go together. If a man can't read, he can't write either.

Writing is not the monopoly of the English Department, and the art of writing should be practiced in all courses, in all departments. The increase in the use of the so-called objective tests—where one has to be able to write nothing except his name, and even that isn't absolutely necessary, for he can now put down his number, if he can remember it—is one of the

---

3) William Faulkner(1897～1962) : 미국 소설가. 주요 작품으로는 *The Sound and the Fury*(1929), *Absalom, Absalom*(1936), *The Bear*(1942) 등이 있음.

4) with discrimination : choosing the best by seeing small differences

alarming indications of a growing illiteracy in our colleges. The president of a well-known liberal arts college in New England recently told his faculty that it was a serious question as to how much longer they continue to call themselves a liberal arts college in view of the general prevalence of the objective test. Well, the English Department at Vanderbilt has never given such a test, and never will. And I hope this is true of other department as well. Answers should be easy answers. A man who can't write a respectable essay isn't an educated man.

A college can have an Honor System[5] only if the spirit of the Honor System is alive among both students and faculty. The Honor System has nothing to do with rules and regulations, trials and retrials, fines and punishments. It withers in an atmosphere of cynicism and distrust. It flourishes only in a climate of mutual trust and loyalty.

It helps a lot to have been brought up in such an atmosphere. But those who haven't been brought up in it can have a change of heart if they honestly desire it. It's a contagious thing, this Honer System. Everyone can rise to it, students and faculty, if they want to. But it is not a matter for debate. It is an outward and visible sign of an inward and spiritual grace. It is an act of faith.

5) Honor System: 무감독 시험제도

A Modest Proposal

Jonathan Swift*

For Preventing the Children of poor People in Ireland, from being a Burden to their Parents of Country; and for making them beneficial to the Public.

It is a melancholy object to those who walk through this great town[1)] or travel in the country, when they see the streets, the roads, and cabin doors crowded with beggars of the female sex, followed by three, four, or six children, all in rags and importuning every passenger for an alms. These mothers, instead of being able to work for

* Jonathan Swift(1667~1745) : Dublin에서 태어난 영국 최대의 풍자작가. 그의 작품으로는 *A Tale of a Tub*(1696), *The Battle of the Books*를 들 수 있으나 대표작은 *The Gulliver's Travels*(1726)이다.

1) 여기서는 Ireland의 Dublin을 말함.

their honest livelihood, are forced to employ all their time in strolling to beg sustenance for their helpless infants, who, as they grow up, either turn thieves for want of work,[2] or leave their dear native country to fight for the Pretender[3] in Spain, or sell themselves to the Barbadoes.[4]

I think it is agreed by all parties[5] that this prodigious number of children in the arms, or on the backs, or at the heels of their mothers, and frequently of their fathers, is in the present deplorable state of the kingdom a very great additional grievance; and, therefore, whoever could find out a fair, cheap, and easy method of making these children sound and useful members of the Commonwealth, would deserve so well of the public as to have his statue set up for a preserver of the nation.

But my intention is very far from[6] being confined to provide only for the children of professed[7] beggars; it is of a much greater extent, and shall take in the whole number of infants at a certain age who are born of parents in effect as little able to support them as those who demand our charity in the streets.

As to my own part, having turned my thoughts for many years upon this important subject, and maturely weighed the several schemes of other pro-

---

2) for want of work : 일자리가 없어서

3) Pretender : 역사상 James Francis Edward 혹은 Stuart(1668~1776)를 가리키나 흔히 어떤 자격을 주장하거나 자격이 있는 체하는 사람을 말함. 여기에서는 왕을 가리킴.

4) sell themselves to the Barbadoes : 서인도제도의 Barbadoes 섬에 자신들을 노예로 팔다.

5) parties : 정당. 여기에서는 영국의 Tory당과 Whig당을 말함.

6) is far from : never

7) professed : 스스로 인정하는, 자인하는

jectors,[8] I have always found them grossly mistaken in their computation. It is true a child, just dropped from its dam[9], may be supported by her milk for a solar year with little other nourishment, at most not above the value of two shillings, which the mother may certainly get, or the value in scraps, by her lawful occupation of begging; and it is exactly at one year old that I propose to provide for them in such a manner as, instead of being a charge upon their parents, or the parish, or wanting food and raiment[10] for the rest of their lives, they shall, on the contrary, contribute to the feeding and partly to the clothing of many thousands.

There is likewise another great advantage in my scheme, that it will prevent those voluntary abortions, and that horrid practice of women murdering their bastard children, alas! too frequent among us!, sacrificing the poor innocent babies, I doubt,[11] more to avoid the expense than the shame, which would move tears and pity in the most savage and inhuman breast.

The number of souls in this kingdom being usually reckoned one million and a half, of these, I calculate there may be about two hundred thousand couples whose wives are breeders;[12] from which number I subtract thirty thousand couples, who are able to maintain their own children, although

---

8) projectors : 인류 복지를 향상시킬 정도로 위대한 사상을 생각해내는 사람들

9) dropped from its dam : 보통 짐승이 새끼를 낳는 경우를 말함. 여기에서는 Jonathan Swift가 인간이 자식을 낳는 일을 비하시키려는 의도를 드러냄.

10) food and raiment : 먹을 것과 입을 것. 성서적 표현임.

11) doubt : "할까 두렵다"의 뜻으로 be afraid, fear의 의미로 쓰임.

12) breeder : 자식을 낳을 수 있는 여자

I apprehend there cannot be so many, under the present distresses of the kingdom; but this being granted, there will remain one hundred and seventy thousand breeders. I again subtract fifty thousand for those women who miscarry, or whose children die by accident or disease within the year. There only remain a hundred and twenty thousand children of poor parents annually born. The question therefore is, how this number shall be reared and provided for? which, as I have already said, under the present situation of affairs, is utterly impossible by all the methods hitherto proposed. For we can neither employ them in handicraft or agriculture; we neither build houses (I mean in the country), nor cultivate land; they can very seldom pick up a livelihood by stealing till they arrive at six years old, except where they are of towardly[13)] parts,[14)] although I confess they learn the rudiments much earlier, during which time, they can, however, be properly looked upon only as probationers, as I have been informed by a principal gentleman in the county of Cavan, who protested to me that he never knew above one or two instances under the age of six, even in a part of the kingdom so renowned for the quickest proficiency in that art.

I am assured by our merchants that a boy or a girl before twelve years old is no saleable commodity, and even when they come to this age they will not yield above three pounds, or three pounds and a half-crown at most on the exchange; which cannot turn to account either to the parents

---

13) towardly(*a*) : 가망성이 있는, 잽싼

14) parts : 소질, 천성

or the kingdom, the charge of nutriment and rags having been at least four times that value.

I shall now therefore humbly propose my own thoughts, which I hope will not be liable to the least objection.

Sex Versus Loveliness

D. H. Lawrence*

It is a pity that sex is such an ugly little word. An ugly little word, and really almost incomprehensible. What is sex, after all? The more we think about it the less we know.

Science says it is an instinct; but what is an instinct? Apparently an instinct is an old, old habit that has become ingrained. But a habit, however old, has to have a beginning. And there is really no beginning to sex. Where life is, there it is. So sex is no "habit" that has been formed.

Again, they talk of sex as an appetite, like hunger. An appetite; but for

---

* D. H. Lawrence(1885～1930) : 영국의 소설가 및 시인. 성문학의 창시자라 일컬어짐. 대표작으로는 *Sons and Lovers*(1913), *The Rainbow*(1915), *Women in Love*(1920), *Lady Chatterley's Lover*(1928) 등이 있다.

what? An appetite for propagation? It is rather absurd. They say a peacock puts on all his fine feathers to dazzle the peahen into letting him satisfy his appetite for propagation. But why should the peahen not put on fine feathers, to dazzle the peacock, and satisfy her desire for propagation? She has surely quite as great a desire for eggs and chickens as he has. We cannot believe that her sex-urge is so weak that she needs all that blue splendour of feathers to rouse her. Not at all.

As for me, I never even saw a peahen so much as look at her lord's bronze and blue glory.[1)] I don't believe she ever sees it. I don't believe for a moment that she knows the difference between bronze, blue, brown or green.

If I had ever seen a peahen gazing with rapt attention on her lord's flamboyancy, I might believe that he had put on all those feathers just to "attract" her. But she never looks at him. Only she seems to get a little perky when he shudders all his quills at her, like a storm in the trees. Then she does seem to notice, just casually, his presence.

These theories of sex are amazing. A peacock puts on his glory for the sake of a wall-eyed peahen who never looks at him. Imagine a scientist being so naive as to credit the peahen with a profound, dynamic appreciation of a peacock's colour and pattern. Oh, highly aesthetic peahen!

And a nightingale sings to attract his female. Which is mighty curious, seeing he sings his best when courtship and honeymoon are over and the

---

1) her lord's bronze and blue glory : 눈이 부실만큼 푸른색과 청동색으로 장식한 숫공작의 모습

female is no longer concerned with him at all, but with the young. Well, then, if he doesn't sing to attract her, he must sing to distract her and amuse her while she's sitting.

How delightful, how naive theories are! But there is a hidden will behind them all. There is a hidden will behind all theories of sex, implacable. And that is the will to deny, to wipe out the mystery of beauty.

Because beauty is a mystery. You can neither eat it nor make flannel out of it. Well, then, says science, it is just a trick to catch the female and induce her to propagate. How naive! As if the female needed inducing. She will propagate in the dark, even — so where, then, is the beauty trick?

Science has a mysterious hatred of beauty, because it doesn't fit in the cause-and-effect chain. And society has a mysterious hatred of sex, because it perpetually interferes with the nice money-making schemes of social man. So the two hatreds made a combine, and sex and beauty are mere propagation appetite.

Now sex and beauty are one thing, like flame and fire. If you hate sex you hate beauty. If you love living beauty, you have a reverence for sex. Of course you can love old, dead beauty and hate sex. But to love living beauty you must have a reverence for sex.

Sex and beauty are inseparable, like life and consciousness. And the intelligence which goes with sex and beauty, and arises out of sex and beauty, is intuition. The great disaster of our civilisation is the morbid hatred of sex. What, for example, could show a more poisoned hatred of sex than Freudian psychoanalysis?—which carries with it a morbid fear of beauty, "alive" beauty, and which causes the atrophy of our intuitive faculty and our intuitive self.

The deep psychic disease of modern men and women is the diseased, atrophied condition of the intuitive faculties. There is a whole world of life that we might know and enjoy by intuition, and by intuition alone. This is denied us, because we deny sex and beauty, the source of the intuitive life and of the insouciance[2)] which is so lovely in free animals and in plants.

Sex is the root of which intuition is the foliage and beauty the flower. Why is a woman lovely, if ever, in her twenties? It is the time when sex rises softly to her face, as a rose to the top of a rose bush.

And the appeal is the appeal of beauty. We deny it wherever we can. We try to make the beauty as shallow and trashy as possible. But, first and foremost, sex appeal is the appeal of beauty.

Now beauty is a thing about which we are so uneducated we can hardly speak of it. We try to pretend it is a fixed arrangement : straight nose, large eyes, etc. We think a lovely woman must look like Lilian Gish,[3)] a handsome man must look like Rudolph Valentino.[4)] So we think.

In actual life we behave quite differently. We say : "She's quite beau-

---

2) insouciance : (F.) indifference;heedlessness

3) Lilian Gish : 1896년 태생의 미국 여배우

4) Rudolph Valentino(1895～1926) : 이탈리아 태생의 미국 영화배우. 성적 매력으로 유명했음.

tiful, but I don't care for her." Which shows we are using the word beautiful all wrong. We should say : "She has the stereotyped attributes of beauty, but she is not beautiful to me."

Beauty is an experience, nothing else. It is not a fixed pattern or an arrangement of features. It is something felt, a glow or a communicated sense of fineness. What ails us is that our sense of beauty is so bruised and blunted, we miss all the best.

But to stick to the films—there is a greater essential beauty in Charlie Chaplin's[5] odd face than ever there was in Valentino's. There is a bit of true beauty in Chaplin's brows and eyes, a gleam of something pure.

But our sense of beauty is so bruised and clumsy, we don't see it, and don't know it when we do see it. We can only see the blatantly obvious, like the so-called beauty of Rudolph Valentino, which only pleases because it satisfies some ready-made notion of handsomeness.

But the plainest person can look beautiful, can be beautiful. It only needs the fire of sex to rise delicately to change an ugly face to a lovely one. That is really sex appeal : the communicating of a sense of beauty.

And in the reverse way, no one can be quite so repellent as a really pretty woman. That is, since beauty is a question of experience, not of concrete form, no one can be as acutely ugly as a really pretty woman. When the sex-glow is missing, and she moves in ugly coldness, how hid-

5) Charlie S. Chaplin(1889～1977) : 영국 출신의 미국 영화배우. 무성영화시대의 희극 배우로서 영화 감독도 겸했다.

eous she seems, and all the worse for her externals of prettiness.

What sex is, we don't know, but it must be some sort of fire. For it always communicates a sense of warmth, of glow. And when the glow becomes a pure shine, then we feel the sense of beauty.

But the communicating of the warmth, the glow of sex, is true sex appeal. We all have the fire of sex slumbering or burning inside us. If we live to be ninety, it is still there. Or, if it dies, we become one of those ghastly living corpses which are unfortunately becoming more numerous in the world.

Nothing is more ugly than a human being in whom the fire of sex has gone out. You get a nasty clayey creature whom everybody wants to avoid.

But while we are fully alive, the fire of sex smoulders or burns in us. In youth it flickers and shines; in age it glows softer and stiller, but there it is. We have some control over it; but only partial control. That is why society hates it.

While ever it lives, the fire of sex, which is the source of beauty and anger, burns in us beyond our understanding. Like actual fire, while it lives it will burn out fingers if we touch it carelessly. And so social man, who only wants to be "safe," hates the fire of sex.

Luckily, not many men succeed in being merely social men. The fire of the old Adam smoulders. And one of the qualities of fire is that it calls to fire. Sex-fire here kindles sex-fire there. It may only rouse the smoulder into a soft glow. It may call up a sharp flicker. Or rouse a flame; and then flame leans to flame, and starts a blaze.

Whenever the sex-fire glows through, it will kindle an answer somewhere or other. It may only kindle a sense of warmth and optimism. Then you say: "I like that girl; she's a real good sort." It may kindle a glow that makes the world look kindlier, and life feel better. Then you say : "She's an attractive woman. I like her."

Or she may rouse a flame that lights up her own face first, before it lights up the universe. Then you say : "She's a lovely woman. She looks lovely to me."

It takes a rare woman to rouse a real sense of loveliness. It is not that a woman is born beautiful. We say that to escape our own poor, bruised, clumsy understanding of beauty. There have been thousands and thousands of women quite as good-looking as Diane de Poitiers,[6] or Mrs. Langtry,[7] or any of the famous ones. There are today thousands and thousands of superbly good-looking women. But oh, how few lovely women!

And why? Because of the failure of their sex appeal. A good-looking woman becomes lovely when the fire of sex rouses pure and fine in her and flickers through her face and touches the fire in me.

Then she becomes a lovely woman to me, then she is in the living flesh a lovely woman : not a mere photograph of one. And how lovely a lovely woman! But, alas! how rare! How bitterly rare in a world full of unusually

6) Diane de Poitiers : 프랑스 Henry II 의 총희

7) Mrs Langtry(1852～1929) : 영국의 여배우. 당시 영국 제일의 미녀

handsome girls and women!

Handsome, good-looking, but not lovely, not beautiful. Handsome and good-looking women are the women with good features and the right hair. But a lovely woman is an experience. It is a question of communicated fire. It is a question of sex appeal in our poor, dilapidated modern phraseology. Sex appeal applied to Diane de Poitiers, or even, in the lovely hours, to one's wife — why, it is a libel and a slander in itself. Nowadays, however, instead of the fire of loveliness, it is sex appeal. The two are the same thing, I suppose, but on vastly different levels.

The business man's pretty and devoted secretary is still chiefly valuable because of her sex appeal. Which does not imply "immoral relations" in the slightest.

Even today a girl with a bit of generosity likes to feel she is helping a man if the man will take her help. And this desire that he shall take her help is her sex appeal. It is the genuine fire, if of a very mediocre heat.

Still, it serves to keep the world of "business" alive. Probably, but for the introduction of the lady secretary into the business man's office, the business man would have collapsed entirely by now. She calls up the sacred fire in her and she communicates it to her boss. He feels an added flow of energy and optimism, and — business flourishes.

There is, of course, the other side of sex appeal. It can be the destruction of the one appealed to. When a woman starts using her sex appeal to her own advantage it is usually a bad moment for some poor devil.[8] But this side of sex appeal has been overworked lately, so it is not nearly as dangerous as it was.

The sex-appealing courtesans who ruined so many men in Balzac no longer find it smooth running.[9] Men have grown canny. They fight shy even of the emotional vamp. In fact, men are inclined to think they smell a rat[10] the moment they feel the touch of feminine sex appeal today.

Which is a pity, for sex appeal is only a dirty name for a bit of life-flame. No man works so well and so successfully as when some woman has kindled a little fire in his veins. No woman does her housework with real joy unless she is in love—and a woman may go on being quietly in love for fifty years almost without knowing it.

If only our civilisation had taught us how to let sex appeal flow properly and subtly, how to keep the fire of sex clear and alive, flickering or glowing or blazing in all its varying degrees of strength and communication, we might, all of us, have lived all our lives in love, which means we should be kindled and full of zest in all kinds of ways and for all kinds of things…

Whereas, what a lot of dead ash there is in life now.

---

8) poor devil : wreched or unfortunate person, 본문에서는 이성(異性)을 뜻하고 있음.

9) no longer find it smooth running : 이제는 남성을 마음대로 주물럭거릴 수 없다. *cf.* run smooth

10) smell a rat : (낌새를)눈치채다, 알아채다

The Boarding House

James Joyce*

Mrs. Mooney was a butcher's daughter. She was a woman who was quite able to keep things to herself[1] : a determined woman. She had married her father's foreman and opened a butcher's shop near Spring Gardens.[2] But as soon as his father-in-law was dead Mr. Mooney began to go to the devil.[3] He drank, plundered the till,[4] ran headlong into debt. It was no use making him take the pledge : he was sure to break out again

* James Joyce(1882~1941) : 영국의 작가. 대표작으로 *Dubliners*(1914)와 *Ulysses*(1922), *Finnegans Wake*(1939)가 있다.

1) keep things to oneself : not disclose things to others

2) Spring Gardens : of Dublin, Ireland

3) go to the devil : be ruined

4) till(*n*) : money box

a few days after. By fighting his wife in the presence of customers and by buying bad meat he ruined his business. One night he went for his wife with the cleaver and she had to sleep in a neighbour's house.

After that they lived apart. She went to the priest and got a separation from him with care of the children. She would give him neither money nor food nor house-room; and so he was obliged to enlist himself as a sheriff's man. He was a shabby stooped little drunkard with a white face and a white moustache and white eyebrows, pencilled above his little eyes, which were pink-veined and raw; and all day long he sat in the bailiff's room, waiting to be put on[5] a job. Mrs. Mooney, who had taken what remained of her money out of the butcher business and set up a boarding house in Hardwicke Street, was a big imposing woman. Her house had a floating population[6] made up of tourists from Liverpool and the Isle of Man and, occasionally, *artistes*[7] from the music halls. Its resident population was made up of clerks from the city. She governed the house cunningly and firmly, knew when to give credit, when to be stern and when to let things pass. All the resident young men spoke of her as *The Madam*.

Mrs. Mooney's young men paid fifteen shillings[8] a week for board and lodgings[9](beer or stout[10] at dinner excluded). They shared in common

---

5) put on : 시키다

6) floating population : 유동 인구 *cf.* resident population

7) *artistes* : (*F*)artists

8) shillings : British silver coin(1/20 sovereign or twelve pence)

9) board and lodgings : 식사 겸한 하숙

10) stout(*n*) : strong beer

tastes and occupations and for this reason they were very chummy with one another. They discussed with one another the chances of favourites and outsiders.[11] Jack Mooney, the Madam's son, who was clerk to a commission agent in Fleet Street, had the reputation of being a hard case.[12] He was fond of using soldiers' obscenities : usually he came home in the small hours.[13] When he met his friends he had always a good one to tell them and he was always sure to be on to a good thing[14]—that is to say, a likely horse or a likely *artiste*. He was also handy with the mitts[15] and sang comic songs. On Sunday nights there would often be a reunion in Mrs. Mooney's front drawing-room. The music-hall *artistes* would oblige; and Sheridan played waltzes and polkas and vamped accompaniments. Polly Mooney, the Madam's daughter, would also sing. She sang :

"I'm a …… naughty girl
You needn't sham :
You know I am."

Polly was a slim girl of nineteen; she had light soft hair and a small full mouth. Her eyes, which were grey with a shade of green through them, had a habit of glancing upwards when she spoke with anyone,

---

11) favourites and outsiders : 인기말과 인기 없는 말
12) hard case : 무뢰한
13) the small hours : early hours of the morning ; 새벽의 1 · 2시경, 숫자가 적으므로
14) be on to a good thing(U.S. Colloq.) : know a good thing
15) handy with the mitts : 주먹질을 잘 하다.

which made her look like a little perverse madonna. Mrs. Mooney had first sent her daughter to be a typist in a corn-factor's office but, as a disreputable sheriff's man used to come every other day to the office, asking to be allowed to say a word to his daughter, she had taken her daughter home again and set her to do housework. As Polly was very lively the intention was to give her the run of the young men. Besides, young men like to feel that there is a young woman not very far away. Polly, of course, flirted with the young men but Mrs. Mooney, who was a shrewd judge, knew that the young men were only passing the time away : none of them meant business. Things went on so for a long time and Mrs. Mooney began to think of sending Polly back to typewriting when she noticed that something was going on between Polly and one of the young men. She watched the pair and kept her own counsel.

Polly knew that she was being watched, but still her mother's persistent silence could not be misunderstood. There had been no open complicity between mother and daughter, no open understanding but, though people in the house began to talk of the affair, still Mrs. Mooney did not intervene. Polly began to grow a little strange in her manner and the young man was evidently perturbed. At last, when she judged it to be the right moment, Mrs. Mooney intervened. She dealt with moral problems as a cleaver deals with meat : and in this case she had made up her mind.

It was a bright Sunday morning of early summer, promising heat, but with a fresh breeze blowing. All the windows of the boarding house were open and the lace curtains ballooned gently towards the street beneath the raised sashes. The belfry of George's Church[16] sent out constant peals and worshippers, singly or in groups, traversed the little circus before the church, revealing their purpose by their self-contained demeanour no less than by the little volumes in their gloved hands. Breakfast was over in the boarding house and the table of the breakfast-room was covered with plates on which lay yellow streaks of eggs with morsels of bacon-fat and bacon-rind. Mrs. Mooney sat in the straw arm-chair and watched the servant Mary remove the breakfast things. She made Mary collect the crusts and pieces of broken bread to help to make Tuesday's bread-pudding. When the table was cleared, the broken bread collected, the sugar and butter safe under lock and key, she began to reconstruct the interview which she had had the night before with Polly. Things were as she had suspected : she had been frank in her questions and Polly had been frank in her answers. Both had been somewhat awkward, of course. She had been made awkward by her not wishing to receive the news in too cavalier a fashion or to seem to have connived, and Polly had been made awkward not merely because allusions of that kind always made her awkward but also because she did not wish it to be thought that in her wise innocence she had divined the intention behind her mother's tolerance.

Mrs. Mooney glanced instinctively at the little gilt clock on the mantelpiece as soon as she had become aware through her revery that the bells of George's Church had stopped ringing. It was seventeen minutes past

---

16) George's Church = *St. George* : patron saint of England from time of Edward Ⅲ

eleven : she would have lots of time to have the matter out with Mr. Doran and then catch short twelve at Marlborough Street. She was sure she would win. To begin with she had all the weight of social opinion on her side : she was an outraged mother. She had allowed him to live beneath her roof, assuming that he was a man of honour, and he had simply abused her hospitality. He was thirty-four or thirty-five years of age, so that youth could not be pleaded as his excuse; nor could ignorance be his excuse since he was a man who had seen something of the world. He had simply taken advantage of Polly's youth and inexperience : that was evident. The question was : What reparation would he make?

There must be reparation made in such cases. It is all very well for the man : he can go his ways as if nothing had happened, having had his moment of pleasure, but the girl has to bear the brunt.[17] Some mothers would be content to patch up such an affair for a sum of money: she had known cases of it. But she would not do so. For her only one reparation could make up for the loss of her daughter's honour : marriage.

She counted all her cards again before sending Mary up to Mr. Doran's room to say that she wished to speak with him. She felt sure she would win. He was a serious young man, not rakish or loud-voiced like the others. If it had been Mr. Sheridan or Mr. Meade or Bantam Lyons, her task would have been much harder. She did not think he would face publicity. All the lodgers in the house knew something of the affair; de-

17) bear the brunt : 전면에 서다.

tails had been invented by some. Besides, he had been employed for thirteen years in a great Catholic wine-merchant's office, and publicity would mean for him, perhaps, the loss of his sit.[18] Whereas if he agreed all might be well. She knew he had a good screw[19] for one thing, and she suspected he had a bit of stuff[20] put by.[21]

Nearly the half-hour! She stood up and surveyed herself in the pier-glass. The decisive expression of her great florid face satisfied her and she thought of some mothers she knew who could not get their daughters off their hands.

Mr. Doran was very anxious indeed this Sunday morning. He had made two attempts to shave but his hand had been so unsteady that he had been obliged to desist. Three days' reddish beard fringed his jaws and every two or three minutes a mist gathered on his glasses so that he had to take them off and polish them with his pocket-handkerchief. The recollection of his confession of the night before was a cause of acute pain to him; the priest had drawn out every ridiculous detail of the affair and in the end had so magnified his sin that he was almost thankful at being afforded a loophole of reparation. The harm was done. What could he do now but marry her or run away? He could not brazen it out.[22] The affair would be sure to be talked of and his employer would be certain to hear of it.

---

18) sit : seat, 여기에서는 job의 뜻
19) screw : salary
20) stuff : money, cash
21) put by : lay up, 간직되어 있다.
22) brazen it out : 시치미를 떼다.

Dublin is such a small city : everyone knows everyone else's business. He felt his heart leap warmly in his throat as he heard in his excited imagination old Mr. Leonard calling out in his rasping voice : "Send Mr. Doran here, please."

All his long years of service gone for nothing! All his industry and diligence thrown away! As a young man he had sown his wild oats,[23] of course; he had boasted of his free-thinking and denied the existence of God to his companions in public-houses. But that was all passed and done with··· nearly. He still bought a copy of *Reynolds's Newspaper* every week, but he attended to his religious duties and for nine-tenths of the year lived a regular life. He had money enough to settle down on; it was not that. But the family would look down on her. First of all there was her disreputable father and then her mother's boarding house was beginning to get a certain fame. He had a notion that he was being had. He could imagaine his friends talking of the affair and laughing. She *was* a little vulgar; sometimes she said "*I seen*" and "*If I had've known*." But what would grammar matter if he really loved her? He could not make up his mind whether to like her or despise her for what she had done. Of course, he had done it too. His instinct urged him to remain free, not to marry. Once you are married you are done for, it said.

While he was sitting helplessly on the side of the bed in shirt and trousers she tapped lightly at his door and entered. She told him all, that she

23) sow his wild oat : indulge in youthful follies

had made a clean breast of it[24] to her mother and that her mother would speak with him that morning. She cried and threw her arms round his neck, saying:

"O Bob! Bob! What am I to do? What am I to do at all?"

She would put an end to herself,[25] she said.

He comforted her feebly, telling her not to cry, that it would be all right, never fear. He felt against his shirt the agitation of her bosom.

It was not altogether his fault that it had happened. He remembered well, with the curious patient memory of the celibate,[26] the first casual caresses her dress, her breath, her fingers had given him. Then late one night as he was undressing for bed she had tapped at his door, timidly. She wanted to relight her candle at his, for hers had been blown out by a gust. It was her bath night. She wore a loose open combing-jacket of printed flannel.[27] Her white instep shone in the opening of her furry slippers and the blood glowed warmly behind her perfumed skin. From her hands and wrists too as she lit and steadied her candle a faint perfume arose.

On nights when he came in very late it was she who warmed up his dinner. He scarcely knew what he was eating, feeling her beside him alone, at night, in the sleeping house. And her thoughtfulness! If the night was anyway cold or wet or windy there was sure to be a little tumbler

---

24) made a clean breast of it : confessed it

25) put an end to herself : kill herself

26) celibate : person resolved not to marry

27) printed flannel : 갱사(更紗) *cf.* printed goods

of punch[28] ready for him. Perhaps they could be happy together…….

They used to go upstairs together on toptoe, each with a candle, and on the third landing exchange reluctant good-nights. They used to kiss. He remembered well her eyes, the touch of her hand and his delirium…….

But delirium passes. He echoed her phrase, applying it to himself : "*What am I to do?*" The instinct of the celibate warned him to hold back. But the sin was there; even his sense of honour told him that reparation must be made for such a sin.

While he was sitting with her on the side of the bed Mary came to the door and said that the missus[29] wanted to see him in the parlour. He stood up to put on his coat and waistcoat, more helpless than ever. When he was dressed he went over to her to comfort her. It would be all right, never fear. He left her crying on the bed and moaning softly : "*O my God!*"

Going down the stairs his glasses became so dimmed with moisture that he had to take them off and polish them. He longed to ascend through the roof and fly away to another country where he would never hear again of his trouble, and yet a force pushed him downstairs step by step. The implacable faces of his employer and of the Madam stared upon his discomfiture. On the last flight of stairs he passed Jack Mooney, who was coming up from the pantry nursing two bottles of *Bass*.[30] They saluted

28) punch(n.) : drink of wine mixed without hot water or milk, sugar, lemon spice etc

29) missus : missis

30) Bass : name of beer made in England, Bass는 양조회사 이름

coldly; and the lover's eyes rested for a second or two on a thick bulldog face and a pair of thick short arms. When he reached the foot of the staircase he glanced up and saw Jack regarding him from the door of the return-room.[31)]

Suddenly he remembered the night when one of the music-hall *artistes*, a little blond Londoner, had made a rather free allusion to Polly. The reunion had been almost broken up on account of Jack's violence. Everyone tried to quiet him. The music-hall *artiste*, a little paler than usual, kept smiling and saying that there was no harm meant; but Jack kept shouting at him that if any fellow tried that sort of a game on with his sister he'd bloody well put his teeth down his throat: so he would.

Polly sat for a little time on the side of the bed, crying. Then she dried her eyes and went over to the looking-glass. She dipped the end of the towel in the water-jug and refreshed her eyes with the cool water. She looked at herself in profile and readjusted a hairpin above her ear. Then she went back to the bed again and sat at the foot. She regarded the pillows for a long time and the sight of them awakened in her mind secret, amiable memories. She rested the nape of her neck against the cool iron bedrail and fell into a revery. There was no longer any perturbation visible on her face.

She waited on patiently, almost cheerfully, without alarm, her memories gradually giving place to hopes and visions of the future. Her hopes and

---

31) return-room : room receding from line of front. 예를 들면 side(room) of house

visions were so intricate that she no longer saw the white pillows on which her gaze was fixed or remembered that she was waiting for anything.

At last she heard her mother calling. She started to her feet and ran to the banisters.

"Polly! Polly!"

"Yes, mamma?"

"Come down, dear. Mr. Doran wants to speak to you."

Then she remembered what she had been waiting for.

Advice to a Young Man

Young men (and women) come to me for advice[1)] about their education and their love affairs.[2)] I try to be generous and kindhearted about my advice.

Good advice sometimes comes too late. We do not find the deep truths of life; they find us.

On Love and Women

Love is the greatest adventure in people's lives. The heart is the noblest part of human nature. And the affections are the noblest ingredients[3)] in human nature.

1) for advice : 조언을 듣기 위해
2) love affair : 애정 문제
3) noblest ingredients : 가장 고상한 구성 요소

Once while hearing a young lady highly praised for her beauty, I asked: What kind of beauty do you mean? Merely that of the body, or also that of the mind? Many a pretty girl is like a flower which is admired for its beautiful appearance, but despised for its unpleasant odor.[4] It is far better to acquire beauty than to be born with it.

No wise person will marry for beauty[5] mainly. It may exercise a powerful attraction[6] in the first place, but it is found to be of comparatively little consequence[7] afterwards. To marry a handsome figure without character,[8] fine features unbeautified by sentiment or good nature, is the most deplorable[9] of mistakes. As even the finest landscape, seen daily, becomes monotonous, so does the most beautiful face, unless a beautiful nature shines through it.

The beauty of today becomes commonplace[10] tomorrow. Whereas goodness, displayed through the most ordinary features,[11] is perennially lovely. This kind of beauty improves with age,[12] and time ripens rather than destroys it.

A man should never be too precisely analytical of a woman.

---

4) unpleasant odor : 유쾌하지 못한 냄새(향)

5) marry for beauty : 미모 때문에 결혼한다.

6) exercise a powerful attraction : 강한 매력을 발휘한다.

7) of little consequence : of little importance 중요하지 않다.

8) figure without character : 인격, 개성이 없는 사람

9) deplorable : 통탄할

10) commonplace : 진부한, 평범한

11) ordinary features : 평범한 외모를 가진 사람

12) with age : 나이가 들어감에 따라

Silence is often the best ornament of a woman.

On Education

I consider ignorance the primary enemy of mankind. The human mind is not only self-destructive[13] but naturally stupid.

Self-ignorance is its normal condition.

The worst fool in the world is the man who will admit nothing that he cannot see or feel or taste, who has no place for imagination or vision or faith.

Man is capable of various kinds of education. He is possessed of[14] physical, social, religious, intellectual and moral capabilities. Each requires education. The education of all makes him complete: the education of part only leaves him deficient.[15]

The educated man is the man who can do something, and the quality of his work marks the degree of his education. The best investment a young man can make[16] is in good books, the study of which broadens the mind.

13) self-destructive : 자기 파괴적인

14) is possessed of : possesses 소유하다

15) deficient : 불완전한, (무엇을) 결하고 있는

16) make investment : 투자를 하다.

On Achieving Success

We cannot travel every path. Success must be won along one line. We must make our business the one life purpose to which every other must be subordinate.[17)]

I hate a thing done by halves.[18)] If it be right, do it boldly: if it be wrong, leave it undone.

To live with ideal is a successful life. It is not what one does, but what one tries to do, that makes a man strong.

"Eternal vigilance,"[19)] it has been said, "is the price of liberty."

With equal truth it may be said, "unceasing effort[20)] is the price of success." If we do not work with our might,[21)] others will: and they will outstrip us in the race, and pluck the prize from our grasp.

Success grows less and less dependent on luck and chance. Self distrust[22)] is the cause of most of our failures.

The great and indispensable help to success is character. Character is crystallized habit,[23)] the result of training and conviction. Every character is influenced by the heredity, environment and education. But these

---

17) subordinate : 종속하는, 부수적인
18) done by halves : 일은 완성시키지 않은 채
19) Eternal vigilance : 끊임없는 주의, 경계
20) unceasing effort : 중단 없는 노력
21) with our might : 힘껏
22) Self distrust : 자기 불신
23) crystallized habit : 결정화(구체화)된 습관

apart,[24] if every man were not to a great extent the architect of his own character, he would be a fatalist, an irresponsible creature of circumstance.[25]

On Happiness

I have never been basically pessimistic, although I have appeared so to some readers. Pessimism is a waster of forces-the penalty of one who doesn't know how to live. Happiness is action, and every power is intended for action. It is a good policy to strike while the iron is hot.[26] It is better still to make the iron hot by striking. I have always found that it's more painful to do nothing than something.

Of all the virtues, cheerfulness and enthusiasm are the most profitable.[27] Enthusiasm flourishes more often in adversity[28] than it does in prosperity. Contentment grows out of[29] an inward superiority to our surroundings. We fall into the mistake of supposing that to look forward must mean to look anxiously forward. It is just as easy to look forward with hope as with sadness.

---

24) these apart : 이런 것들을 제외하고라도
25) irresponsible creature of circumstance : 주변 환경에 의해 형성된 무책임한 사람
26) It is a good policy to strike while the iron is hot : 쇠는 뜨겁게 달았을 때 치라는 속담으로 기회가 왔을 때 잡으라는 의미임.
27) profitable : 이익이 되는, 중요한
28) in adversity : 역경에 처해서
29) grows out of : ~로부터 생겨나다.

Meeting the Perfect Mate

For the past month I've been taking a graduate seminar[1] called "Social Structure." It's a very popular course.[2] We've been discussing friendship, marriage, and other relationships. One of our assignments[3] is to examine the ways that people meet potential husbands and wives.[4] I've been interviewing students on campus all week as part of my study.

First, I talked with my roommate in the dormitory,[5] Sook In, a student from Korea.

"What's one way to meet a possible mate?" I asked her.

"Well," she said, "one method in my country is to have a matched

1) taking a graduate seminar : 대학원과정의 세미나 강좌를 수강하다.
2) course : 대학(원)의 강좌
3) assignments : 과제
4) potential husbands and wives : (결혼하지 않은 미혼들이) 장차 맞이하게 될 남편, 아내
5) dormitory : 기숙사, on-campus dormitory 학교 내 기숙사; off-dormitory 교외 기숙사

marriage."[6]

"A what?" I asked. "I know you can match a tie to a shirt-or two socks after you do the laundry. But people?"

"Sure," she replied. "There aren't many arranged marriages these days, but there were a lot not too long ago. Many parents, for examples, met each other for the first time on their wedding day. My grandparents chose their children's mates and arranged[7] the wedding."

"Do you mean that they weren't in love? That sounds awful![8] Weren't they upset?"

"Maybe a little bit," Sook In said, "But they accepted each other. Then, fortunately, they grew to love each other. They've had a good, successful marriage for the past thirty years. This happens in a lot of arranged marriages."

I shock my head. "Amazing!" I said.

The next person that I interviewed was Bill, a guy in my business management class.[9]

"I meet a lot of women in nightclubs—at least more than I do on campus," he said. "The environment[10] is exciting and I go every weekend, if possible, to dance or talk or just listen to music."

"That seems great," I said.

---

6) matched marriage : 중매결혼
7) arrange : 주선하다
8) That sounds awful! : 정말 끔찍하군!
9) business management class : 경영학 수업반
10) environment : 주변 환경

"I thought so, too, at first," he said a little sadly. "But on the other hand, very often the women in those places are unfriendly. A lot of men are too aggressive,[11)] and as a result the women are very cold."

"Nightclubs? Never!" said Julia, a student who works part-time[12)] in the campus bookstore. "I prefer to make new friends at places where people have interests in common.[13)] I met my boyfriend at the health club, for example, and it seems that the healthy atmosphere of the gym is continuing into the relationship that I have with him."

"That sounds wonderful," I said.

"Yes," she said, "I guess so. But to be honest, there's one problem with this arrangement."

"What?" I asked.

"The truth is that I really hate to exercise, so I don't want to go to the gym anymore. What's my boyfriend going to think when he finds this out?"

"Computer dating services are the answer!" said my friend Sara, who lives down the hall from me in the dormitory. "They provide a great way to meet people! The biggest advantage is that you have a lot in common with the people you meet through a computer. The computer can match you up with someone of your same intelligence, astrological[14)] sign, age,

---

11) aggressive : 공격적인

12) work part time : 시간제로 일하다, 아르바이트(arbeit)는 일하다라는 의미의 독일어이다.

13) interests in common : 공통된 흥미, 관심사항을 갖다.

14) astrological : 점성술의

lifestyle, and personality. For instance, you can meet someone who is creative, competitive, and honest, and you can ask for a scientist, an actor, a vegetarian,[15) or . . ."

"Have you had many successful dates so far?" I asked.

"To tell the truth," she said, "no, I think I made a big mistake when I filled out the application form.[16) I didn't want to miss a wonderful guy because of an answer that was too specific, so I was careful to write very general answers."

"What do you mean?"

"Well, there was a question about height. I said 'anyone between 3'5" and 7'5"' Then there was a question about recreation. I answered 'yes' to forty-seven interests, from gourmet[17) cooking to camping in the wilderness.

I wrote that I liked swimming, hiking, the arts, comedy movies, quiz shows,[18) mystery stories, business, ethic foods,[19) and so on, but I think that the computer got confused. It hasn't found a date for me since I sent in the application."

"And what about video dating?" asked Sara's roommate, Sandra.

"Dating by video?" I asked. "How is that possible?"

"Well, I haven't done it myself because it's expensive. But I've seen the

---

15) vegetarian : 채식주의자

16) fill out the application form : 신청서류를 작성하다.

17) gourmet : 미식가

18) quiz show : 여러 사람이 나와 퀴즈 문제를 알아 맞추는 미국에서 인기 있는 TV프로그램이다

19) ethic food : 미국에 이주해온 여러 민족들의 고유한 음식

ads[20] and in the newspaper. You join a video-dating club. They film you as you talk about yourself . . . you know, your background and your interests and things like that. Then you view videotapes of men, and if you want to meet someone, you write his membership number on a computer form. Then he sees *your* video, and if he likes what he sees on the screen . . . you arrange to meet!"

"Hmm . . .," I answered. "More television in your life"

"Well, you could place a personal ad,[21]" Sandra continued.

"In the newspaper?"

"Sure. A friend of mine did that. He wanted to get married, so he figured out the statistics.[22] He decided that out of every ten women, he liked one. And out of every ten women he liked, he might fall in love with one. Therefore, to get married, he just needed to meet one hundred women."

"Did it work?" I asked.

There was no answer.

Last I interviewed a guy in the cafeteria.

"Supermarkets," he told me.

"You're kidding," I said.

"No, I'm serious. I meet a lot of potential dates over the frozen pizzas in the convenience-food section.[23] Also, it's easy to make small talk over

---

20) ads : advertisements 광고

21) place a personal ad : 자신에 관한 광고를 내다.

22) figured out the statistics : 통계를 내어보다.

23) the convenience-food section : supermarket의 인스턴트식품을 모아 놓은 곳

the tomatoes and lettuce in the produce section.[24] We discuss chemicals and nutrition and food prices. Sometimes this leads to a very romantic date." I slowly shook my head: It is strange . . . very strange. I bit my lip because I didn't want to be impolite.

That evening, I talked with my roommate, Sook In.

"You know," I said. "I think maybe your parents and grandparents had a pretty good idea. A matched marriage is beginning to seem more and more practical to me."

24) produce section : 농산물을 모아 놓은 곳 (야채부)

Thank You, Ma'm

Langston' Hughes*

She was a large woman with a large purse that had everything in it but a hammer and nails. It had a long strap, and she carried it slung across her shoulder. It was about eleven o'clock at night, dark, and she was walking alone, when a boy ran up behind her and tried to snatch her purse. The strap broke with the sudden single tug the boy gave it from behind. But the boy's weight and the weight of the purse combined caused him to lose his balance. Instead of taking off full blast[1] as he had hoped, the boy fell on his back on the sidewalk and his legs flew up.[2] The large

---

* 미국의 흑인 시인, 소설가

1) full blast : 전속력으로

2) his legs flew up : 엉덩방아를 찧다.

woman simply turned around and kicked him until his teeth rattled.

After that the woman said, "Pick up my pocketbook, boy, and give it here."

She still held him tightly. But she bent down enough to permit him to stoop and pick up her purse. Then she said, "Now ain't you ashamed of yourself?"

Firmly gripped by his shirt front, the boy said, "Yes'm."[3)]

The woman said, "What did you want to do it for?"

The boy said, "I didn't aim to.[4)]"

By that time two or three people passed, stopped, turned to look, and some stood watching.

"If I turn you loose, will you run?" asked the woman.

"Yes'm," said the boy.

"Then I won't turn you loose," said the woman. She did not release him.

"Lady, I'm sorry," whispered the boy.

"Um-hum! Your face is dirty. I got a great mind[5)] to wash your face for you. Ain't you got nobody home to tell you to wash your face?"

"No'm," said the boy.

"Then it will get washed this evening," said the large woman, starting up the street, dragging the frightened boy behind her.

He looked as if he were fourteen or fifteen, frail and willow-wild in ten-

---

3) Yes'm : Yes, ma'm

4) aim to : plan to

5) I got a great mind : 대단히 ~ 하고 싶다.

nis shoes and blue jeans.

The woman said, "You ought to be my son. I would teach you right from wrong. Least I can do right now is to wash your face. Are you hungry?"

"No'm," said the being-dragged boy. "I just want you to turn me loose."

"Was I bothering you when I turned that corner?" asked the woman.

"No'm,"

"But you put yourself in contact with me," said the woman. "If you think that that contact is not going to last awhile, you got another thought coming.[6] When I get through with you, sir, you are going to remember Mrs. Luella Bates Washington Jones."

Sweat popped out[7] on the boy's face and he began to struggle. Mrs. Jones stopped, jerked him around in front of her, put a half-nelson[8] about his neck, and continued to drag him up the street. When she got to her door, she dragged the boy inside, down a hall, and into a large kitchenette-furnished room[9] at the rear of the house. She switched in the light and left the door open. The boy could hear other roomers laughing and talking in the large house. Some of their doors were open, too, so he knew he and the woman were not alone. The woman still had him by the neck in the middle of her room.

6) you got another thought coming : you had better think again

7) popped out : 튀어나오다

8) put a half-nelson : 단단히 움켜쥐다.

9) kitchenette-furnished room : 작은 부엌과 가구가 설비된 아파트

She said, "What is your name?"

"Roger," answered the boy.

"Then, Roger, you go to that sink and wash your face," said the woman, whereupon she turned him loose — at last. Roger looked at the door — looked at the woman — looked at the door — and went to the sink.

"Let the water run until it gets warm," she said. "Here's a clean towel."

"You gonna[10] take me to jail?" asked the boy, bending over the sink.

"Now with that face, I would not take you nowhere," said the woman. "Here I am trying to get home to cook me a bite to eat, and you snatch my pocketbook? Maybe you ain't been to your supper either, late as it be. Have you?"

"There's nobody home at my house," said the boy.

"Then we'll eat," said the woman, "I believe you're hungry — or been hungry — to try to snatch my pocketbook!"

"I want a pair of blue suede shoes," said the boy.

"Well, you didn't have to snatch my pocketbook to get some suede shoes," said Mrs. Luella Bates Washington Jones. "You could have asked me."

"Ma'm?"

The water dripping from his face, the boy looked at her. There was a long pause. A very long pause. After he had dried his face and not knowing what else to do, dried it again, the boy turned around, wondering what

10) gonna : going to

next. The door was open. He would make a dash for it down the hall. He would run, run, run!

The woman was sitting on the day-bed.[11] After a while, she said, "I was young once and I wanted things I could not get."

There was another long pause. The boy's mouth opened. Then he frowned not knowing he frowned.

The woman said, "Um-hum! You thought I was going to say but, didn't you? You thought I was going to say, but I didn't snatch people's pocketbooks. Well, I wasn't going to say that." Pause. Silence. "I have done things, too, which I would not tell you, son-neither tell God, if he didn't already know. Everybody's got something in common. Sit you down while I fix us something to eat. You might run that comb through your hair[12] so you will look presentable."

In another corner of the room behind a screen was a gas plate and an icebox. Mrs. Jones got up and went behind the screen. The woman did not watch the boy to see if he was going to run now, nor did she watch her purse, which she left behind her on the day bed. But the boy took care to sit on the far side of the room, away from the purse, where he tought she could easily see him out of the corner of her eye if she wanted to. He did not trust the woman to trust him.[13] And he did not want to be mistrusted now.

11) day-bed : 침대로 사용할 수 있는 소파

12) run that comb ~ hair : 빗으로 머리를 빗어라.

13) He did not trust the woman not to trust him : He wanted her to trust him.

"Do you need somebody to go to the store," asked the boy, "maybe to get some milk or something?"

"Don't believe I do," said the woman, "unless you just want sweet milk yourself. I was going to make cocoa out of this canned milk I got here."

She heated some lima beans[14)] and ham she had in the icebox, made the cocoa, and set the table. The woman did not ask the boy anything about where he lived, or his folks, or anything else that would embarrass him. Instead, as they ate, she told him about son in[15)] a hotel beauty shop that stayed open late, what the work was like, and how all kinds of woman came in and out, blondes, redheads and Spanish. Then she cut him half of her ten-cent cake.

"Eat some more, son," she said.

When they finished eating, she got up and said, "Now here, take this ten dollars and buy yourself some blue suede shoes. And, next time, do not make the mistake of latching onto my pocketbook nor nobody else's—because shoes got by devilish ways will burn your feet. I got to get my rest now. But from here on in,[16)] son, I hope you will behave yourself."

She led the way down the hall to the front door and opened it. "Good night! Behave yourself, boy!" she said, looking into the street as he went down the steps.

The boy wanted to say something other than "Thank you, ma'm," to

---

14) lima beans : 납작한 푸른 콩
15) here on in : 앞으로
16) from here on in : 앞으로는

Mrs. Luella Bates Washington Jones, but although his lips moved, he couldn't even say that, as he turned at the foot of the barren stoop and looked up at the large woman in the door. Then she shut the door.

Is Love an Art?

Erich Fromm*

Is love an art? Then it requires knowledge and effort. Or is love a pleasant sensation, which to experience is a matter of chance, something one "falls into" if one is lucky? This essay is based on the former premise, while undoubtedly the majority of people today believe in the latter.

Not that[1] people think that love is not important. They are starved for[2] it; they watch endless numbers of films about happy and unhappy love sto-

* Erich Fromm(1900~1980): 독일의 심리학자, 사회학자. 정신분석학과 사회심리학 분야에 다수의 저서를 출간.

1) Not that : ~이라는 것은 아니다.

2) are starved for : 갈구하다, 굶주리다

ries, they listen to hundred of trashy songs about love—yet hardly anyone thinks that there is anything that needs to be learned about love.

This peculiar attitude is based on several premises which either singly or combined tend to uphold[3] it. Most people see the problem of love primarily as that of *being loved*, rather than that of *loving*, of one's capacity to love. Hence the problem to them is how to be loved, how to be lovable. In pursuit of this aim they follow several paths. One, which is especially used by men, is to be successful, to be as powerful and rich as the social margin of one's position permits. Another, used especially by women, is to make oneself attractive, by cultivating one's body, dress, etc. Other ways of making oneself attractive, used both by men and women, are to develop pleasant manners, interesting conversation, to be helpful, modest, inoffensive. Many of the ways to make oneself lovable are the same as those used to make oneself successful, "to win friends and influence people." As a matter of fact, what most people in our culture mean by being lovable is essentially a mixture between being popular and having sex appeal.

A second premise behind the attitude that there is nothing to be learned about love is the assumption[4] that the problem of love is the problem of an object, not the problem of a faculty. People think that to love is simple, but that to find the right object to love—or to be loved by—is difficult.

3) uphold : 지지하다

4) assumption : 가정

This attitude has several reasons rooted in the development of modern society. One reason is the great change which occurred in the twentieth century with respect to[5] the choice of a "love object." In the Victorian age, as in many traditional cultures, love was mostly not a spontaneous personal experience which then might lead to marriage. On the contrary, marriage was contracted by convention—either by the respective families, or by a marriage broker, or without the help of such intermediaries,[6] it was concluded on the basis of social considerations, and love was supposed to develop once the marriage had been concluded. In the last few generations the concept of romantic love has become almost universal in the Western world. In the United States, while considerations of a conventional nature are not entirely absent, to a vast extent[7] people are in search of "romantic love," of the personal experience of love which then should lead to marriage. This new concept of freedom in love must have greatly enhanced the importance of the object as against the importance of the function.

Closely related to this factor is another feature characteristic of contemporary culture. Our whole culture is based on the appetite for buying, on the idea of a mutually favorable exchange. Modern man's happiness consists in the thrill of looking at the shop windows, and in buying all that he can afford to buy, either for cash or on installments.[8] He(or she) looks

5) with respect to : ~에 관하여
6) intermediaries : 중매자
7) a vast extent : 광범위하게

at people in a similar way. For the man an attractive girl—and for the woman an attractive man—are the prizes they are after.[9] "Attractive" usually means a nice package of qualities[10] which are popular and sought after on the personality market. What specifically makes a person attractive depends on the fashion of the time, physically as well as mentally. During the twenties, a drinking and smoking girl, tough and sexy, was attractive; today the fashion demands more domesticity[11] and coyness. At the end of the nineteenth and the beginning of this century, a man had to be aggressive and ambitious—today he has to be social and tolerant—in order to be an attractive "package." At any rate, the sense of falling in love develops usually only with regard to such human commodities as are within reach of one's own possibilities for exchange. I am out for a bargain;[12] the object should be desirable from the standpoint of its social value, and at the same time should want me, considering my overt and hidden assets and potentialities. Two persons thus fall in love when they feel they have found the best object available on the market, considering the limitations of their own exchange values. Often, as in buying real estate, the hidden potentialities which can be developed play a considerable role in this bargain. In a culture in which the marketing orientation prevails, and in which material success is the outstanding value, there is little reason to be

---

8) installments : 분할불

9) the prize they are after : 그들이 추구하는 상품

10) a nice package of qualities : 일괄적으로 훌륭한 자질

11) domesticity : 가정적임

12) I am out for a bargain : 흥정하려고 나섰다.

surprised that human love relations follow the same pattern of exchange which governs the commodity and the labor market.

The third error leading to the assumption that there is nothing to be learned about love lies in the confusion between the initial experience of "*falling*" in love, and the permanent state of *being* in love, or as we might better say, of "standing" in love. If two people who have been strangers, as all of us are, suddenly let the wall between them break down, and feel close, feel one, this moment of oneness is one of the most exhilarating,[13] most exciting experiences in life. It is all the more wonderful and miraculous for persons who have been shut off, isolated, without love. This miracle of sudden intimacy is often facilitated[14] if it is combined with, or initiated by, sexual attraction and consummation. However, this type of love is by its very nature not lasting. When the two persons become well acquainted, their intimacy loses more and more its miraculous character, until their antagonism,[15] their disappointments, their mutual boredom kill whatever is left of the initial excitement. Yet, in the beginning they do not know all this : in fact, they take the intensity of the infatuation, this being "crazy" about each other, for proof of the intensity of their love, while it may only prove the degree of their preceding loneliness.

This attitude—that nothing is easier than to love—has continued to be the prevalent idea about love in spite of the overwhelming evidence to the

---

13) exhilarating : 생기를 돋우어 주는

14) be facilitated : 쉽게 이루어지다.

15) antagonism : 적대감

contrary. There is hardly any activity, any enterprise, which is started with such tremendous hopes and expectations, and yet, which fails so regularly, as love. If this were the case with any other activity, people would be eager to know the reasons for the failure, and to lean how one could do better—or they would give up the activity. Since the latter is impossible in the case of love, there seems to be only one adequate way to overcome the failure of love—to examine the reasons for this failure, and to proceed to study the meaning of love.

The first step to take is to become aware that love is an art, just as living is an art; if we want to learn how to love we must proceed in the same way we have to proceed if we want to learn any other art, say music, painting, carpentry, or the art of medicine or engineering.

What are the necessary steps in learning any art?

The process of learning an art can be divided conveniently into two parts: one, the mastery of the theory; the other, the mastery of the practice. If I want to learn the art of medicine, I must first know the facts about the human body, and about various diseases. When I have all the theoretical knowledge, I am by no means competent in the art of medicine. I shall become a master in this art only after a great deal of practice, until eventually the results of my theoretical knowledge and the results of my practice are blended into one—my intuition, the essence of the mastery of any art. But, aside from learning the theory and practice, there is a third factor necessary to becoming a master in any art—the mastery of the art must be a matter of ultimate concern;[16)] there must be nothing else in the world more important than the art. This holds true for music, for medicine, for carpentry—and for love. And maybe, here lies the answer to the question of why people in our culture try so rarely to learn this art, in spite of their obvious failure : in spite of the deep-seated craving[17] for love, almost everything else is considered to be more important than love : success, prestige,[18] money, power—almost all our energy is used for the learning of how to achieve these aims, and almost none to learn the art of loving.

Could it be that only those things are considered worthy of being learned with which one can earn money or prestige, and that love, which "only" profits the soul, but is profitless in the modern sense, is a luxury we have no right to spend much energy on?

16) ultimate concern : 궁극적 관심

17) the deep-seated craving : 깊이 박힌 갈망

18) prestige : 명성

Appointment with Love

S. I. Kishor*

Six minutes to six, said the great round clock over the information booth in Grand Central Station.[1)] The tall young Army lieutenant who had just come from the direction of the tracks lifted his sunburned face, and his eyes narrowed to note the exact time. His heart was pounding with a beat that shocked him because he could not control it. In six minutes, he would see the woman who had filled such a special place in his life for the past thirteen months, the woman he had never seen, yet whose written words had been with him and sustained him unfailingly.

---

* S. I. Kishor: 미국 단편 소설 작가.

1) Grand Central Station : New York시 Upper Manhattan의 종착역

He placed himself as close as he could to the information booth, just beyond the ring of people besieging the clerks…….

Lieutenant Blandford remembered one night in particular, the worst of the fighting, when plane had been caught in the midst of a pack of Zeros.[2] He had seen the grinning face of one of the Jap[3] pilots.

In one of his letters, he had confessed to her that he often felt fear, and only a few days before this battle, he had received her answer : "Of course, you fear…… all brave men do. Didn't King David[4] know fear? That's why he wrote the Twenty-third Psalm.

Next time you doubt yourself I want you to hear my voice reciting to you : "Yea, though I walk in the valley of the shadow of death, I shall fear no evil, for thou art with me[5]……." And he had remembered he had heard her imagined voice, and it had renewed his strength and skill.

Now he was going to hear her real voice. Four minutes to six. His face grew sharp.

Under the immense, starred roof,[6] people were walking fast, like threads of color being woven into a gray web. A girl passed close to him, and Lieutenant Blandford started.[7] She was wearing a red flower in her suit

---

2) Zeros: 제2차 세계대전 때 일본군이 사용한 전투기. 제작연대(일본연대) 2600(=1949 A.D.)년의 0자를 딴 것.

3) Jap : Japanese

4) King David : 이스라엘의 제2대왕으로 시편의 저자.

5) "Yea, though I walk …… with me" : Psalm 23 : 4

6) the immense, starred roof : the big roof of the Central Station illuminated with many lights

7) started : was startled

lapel, but it was a crimson sweet pea, not the little red rose they had agreed upon. Besides, this girl was too young, about eighteen, whereas Hollis Meynell had frankly told him she was thirty. "Well, what of it?"[8] He had answered. "I'm thirty-two." He was twenty-nine.

His mind went back to that book—the book the Lord Himself must have put into his hand out of the hundreds of Army library books sent to the Florida training camp. *Of Human Bondage*[9], it was; and throughout the book were notes in a woman's writing. He had always hated that writing-in habit[10], but these remarks were different. He had never believed that a woman could see into a man's heart so tenderly, so understandingly. Her name was on the bookplate : Hollis Meynell. He had got hold of a New York City telephone book and found her address. He had written, she had answered. Next day he had been shipped out, but they had gone on writing. For thirteen months, she had faithfully replied, and more than replied. When his letters did not arrive, she wrote anyway, and now he believed he loved her, and she loved him.

But she had refused all his pleas to send him her photograph. That seemed rather bad, of course. But she had explained : "If your feeling for me has any reality, any honest basis, what I look like won't matter. Suppose I'm beautiful, I'd always be haunted by the feeling that you had

---

8) what of it? : so what?, that is of no importance

9) Of Human Bondage : William S, Maugham의 자전적 소설

10) writing-in habit : 책에 적어 넣는 버릇

been taking a chance on just that,[11] and that kind of love would disgust me. Suppose I'm plain,[12] (and you must admit that this is more likely) then I'd always fear that you were only going on writing to me because you were lonely and had no one else. No, don't ask for my picture. When you come to New York, you shall see me and then you shall make your decision. Remember, both of us are free to stop or to go on after that—whichever we choose ……."

One minute to six … he pulled hard on a cigarette.[13]

The Lieutenant Blandford's heart leaped higher than his plane had ever done.

A young woman was coming toward him. Her figure was long and slim; her blond hair lay back in curls from her delicate ears. Her eyes were blue as flowers, her lips and chin had a gentle firmness. In her pale green suit, she was like springtime come alive.

He started toward her, entirely forgetting to notice that she was wearing no rose, and as he moved, a small, provocative smile curved her lips.

"Going my way,[14] soldier?" she murmured.

Uncontrollably, he made one step closer to her. Then he saw Hollis Meynell.

She was standing almost directly behind the girl, a woman well past for-

---

11) just that : the fact that I am beautiful

12) plain : not good-looking, homely

13) pulled hard on a cigarette : 담배를 힘껏 빨았다.

14) Going my way……? : Are you going my way……?

ty, her graying hair tucked under a worn hat. She was more than plump; her thick-ankled feet were thrust into lowheeled shoes. But she wore a red rose in the rumpled brown lapel of her coat.

The girl in the green suit was walking quickly away.

Blandford felt as though he was being split in two, so keen was his desire to follow the girl, yet so deep was his longing for the woman whose spirit had truly companioned and upheld his own; and there she stood. Her pale, plump face was gentle and sensible; he could see that now. Her gray eyes had a warm, kindly twinkle.

Lieutenant Blandford did not hesitate. His fingers gripped the small, worn, blue leather copy of *Of Human Bondage* which was to identify him to her. This would not be love, but it would be something precious, something perhaps even rarer than love — a friendship for which he had been and must ever be grateful…….

He squared his broad shoulders, saluted and held the book out toward the woman, although even while he spoke he felt chocked by the bitterness of his disappointment.

"I'm Lieutenant John Blandford, and you — you are Miss Meynell. I'm so glad you could meet me. May — may I take you to dinner?"

The woman's face broadened in a tolerant smile. "I don't know what this is all about, son." she answered. "That young lady in the green suit, who just went by, begged me to wear this rose on my coat. And she said that if you asked me to go out with you, I should tell you that she's waiting for you in that big restaurant across the street. She said it was some kind of a test. I've got[15] two boys with Uncle Sam[16] myself, so I didn't mind to oblige you."[17]

15) I've got : I have
16) Uncle Sam : the U.S. Government
17) oblige you : do a favor for you

Mamie

Hans Zinsser

The first girl I ever noticed in what, later, I recognized as a sentimental emotion was called Mamie. She was the daughter of a truck driver in my father's chemical factory. We used to play in the large factory yard, where hundreds of barrels of resin were stored on end, and it was great fun to jump from barrel top to barrel top. Mamie had a brother who became a bosom friend, and games of tag on the barrels were organized in which Mamie — being several years younger — was patronizingly allowed to participate. She and her brother were sweet children, amiable and gentle, and I loved them both very dearly. Their lives were hard. At twelve and ten respectively, they were called upon[1] for severe

1) were called upon : 요구 당했다.

domestic service, and their poor mother—a stout, red-faced woman—kind enough when she was sober, was less so when drunk. Their happy moments were the ones they spent with me, playing on the barrels; but when I went back to my play-room to have my feet dried and to be fed my supper, they went back to a little frame house where dirt, noise, unmerited abuse, and frugal tolerance were their lot.

Mamie was blue-eyed and blonde, with a bright blondeness that shone through the dirt on her face and the squalor of her clothes. And how humbly grateful she was to be allowed to be "It", chasing us over the barrels. There must have been a faint dawning of the endocrines[2)] in me even then, for while I was sorry for Jimmy when I happened to think of being so,[3)] there was always a protective tenderness in my heart for Mamie.

One day—it was drizzling—the wet drove us from our playground into a little shed where carboys of sulphuric acid were stored. I dug a nickel out of my pocket and Jimmy was dispatched to the store on the corner to buy some barber-pole candy sticks.[4)] Mamie and I sat close together, for we were damp and a little chilly. She stuck up her wet face to be kissed, and I gazed down at her with the warm intention of kissing her. But when I looked into her face, I saw two little rivulets running from Mamie's nose to her pouted upper lip. I had never noticed them before, although I had often observed her sticking her tongue out and upward,

---

2) a faint dawning of endocrines : 연애 감정의 시초

3) when I happened … so : 어쩌다 안됐다는 생각이 들 때에

4) barber-pole candy sticks : 빨갛고 흰줄이 있는 막대기로 된 사탕

whenever she sniffed. For ours was a catarrhal climate. Now I looked and saw. But I have always been proud in later days that, even at this early age, I mastered my repulsion and kissed Mamie on her salty lips.

Dear Mamie! What has become of you since? You were a lovely child, in spite of the rivulets on your upper lip, and—no doubt—you deserved more consideration than the world has given you. What happened to me at that moment has never left me since[5] and is perhaps the only achievement that may eventually entitle me to some measure of self-approbation[6] —namely, the mastery of arrogance and disgust by tenderness and pity.

We played in the great court of my father's chemical factory and the atmosphere was redolent with odors of resin,[7] sulphuric acid and amyl acetate. I never pass a chemical factory or smell amyl acetate without thinking of Mamie and our games on the barrels. Yes, the sense of smell is the most nostalgic of our senses.

5) never left me since : 그 이후로 잊는 일이 없다.
6) that may … self-approbation : 어느 정도 자기가 잘했다고 인정할 자격을 줄 수 있는
7) redolent with odors of resin : 송진 냄새가 진동하다.

The Show Must Go On!

Harry Golden

I love the theatre and everybody connected with it, from actor to stagehand. I believe however that this buisness of "the show must go on"[1] has been overdone a bit[2] as it[3] concerns the acting profession.[4] Not that[5] I doubt the truth behind this tradition.[6] I know very well that performers have faced their audiences with deep sorrow in their hearts ;

1) the show must go on : "연기는 계속되어야 한다". 이 말은 연기자들의 활동에 긍지를 나타낼 때 즐겨 사용하여 온 말. 개인의 사정보다도 직책이 우선한다는 뜻.

2) a bit : 다소

3) it : this business

4) as it concerns the acting profession : 연기가 직업인 때문에

5) not that ~ : ~라는 말은 아니다.

6) this tradition : 이 구호의 전통

with news of some terrible personal disaster, and as in *Pagliacci*[7] the clown[8] bravely goes on with the show: "Laugh with the sorrow that's breaking your heart." I rise up to applaud. But I do not applaud actors alone. I applaud people. All people. Life itself. Everybody goes out on the "stage" with sorrow in his heart. For everybody, the show must go on. How many workingmen have come home from the cemetery where they had just buried a child and sat right down at their workbenches, machines, and lathes? How many house-wives pitch in[9] to get the children ready for school, do the marketing and household chores, with breaking backs, migraine headaches, and perhaps a personal sorrow, too? THE SHOW MUST GO ON. Not only for actors, but for all of us.[10] We dare not stop "the show" for a single moment.

A few days after my mother died I was behind the counter[11] of my brother's hotel and a guest bawled me out[12] because his laundry hadn't come back on time. For a fleeting moment[13] I had foolishly expected the world to stand still[14] and pay homage to my mother. I checked my mounting anger in the nick of time.[15] "Of course," I said, "this man is

---

7) *Pagliacci* : Leoncavallo의 오페라(1892)
8) the clown : 광대, 여기서는 오페라에 등장하는 테너가수 Canio를 말함.
9) pitch in : 일을 시작하다.
10) all of us : 세상 모든 사람들
11) behind the counter : 계산대 뒤에
12) bawl out : 꾸짖다
13) fleeting moment : 순간
14) stand still : 우뚝 멈추다.
15) in the nick of time : 알맞은 때에. 여기에서는 "폭발 직전에"라는 뜻.

blameless. He's interested in his laundry—he's interested in now, in living, in life."

I am indebted to[16] Dr. Frank Kingdon for my interest in the poetry of Sir Rabindranath Tagore. The great Hindu poet tells us a story in exquisite poetry. His servant did not come in on time. Like so many philosophers and poets, Tagore was helpless when it came to[17] the less important things[18] in life, his personal wants, his clothes, his breakfast, and tidying up the place. An hour went by and Tagore was getting madder by the minute.[19] He thought of all sorts of punishments for the man. Three hours later Tagore no longer thought of punishment. He'd discharge the man without any further ado,[20] get rid of him, turn him out. Finally the man showed up.[21] It was midday. Without a word the servant proceeded with[22] his duties as though nothing had happened. He picked up his master's clothes, set to[23] making breakfast, and started cleaning up. Tagore watched this performance with mounting rage. Finally he said it: "Drop everything, and get out."

The man, however, continued sweeping, and after another few moments, with quiet dignity he said: "My little girl died last night."

The show must go on.

---

16) am indebted to ~ : ~에게 은혜를 입고 있다.
17) when it came to ~ : ~의 문제를 당하면
18) less important things : 덜 중요한 일들 : 시인에게는 시 창작이 가장 중요한 일.
19) by the minute : 매 분 단위로, 즉 화가 높아가는 정도가 분 단위로 갈라진다는 뜻.
20) without any further ado : 더 이상 소란 피울 것 없이.
21) show up : 나타나다.
22) proceed with ~ : ~을 계속하다.
23) set to ~ing : ~하기 시작하다.

From Aesop's *Fables*

Aesop*

The Lion and Other Beasts Go Hunting

One day, tired of hunting by himself, the lion gathered some other beasts together suggested they go on a hunt. Proud to be at the side of such a great hunter, the other beasts were happy to join him. The hunters cornered[1)] and killed a fat juicy stag. The lion stood over the fallen prey.

"Beasts," he roared, "We shall now divide the spoils fairly. First, the

---

* Aesop : 『이솝이야기』의 작자로서, Aesop은 Aisopos의 영어식 표기로 BC 6세기경의 사람이다. 사모아사람인 이아도몬의 노예였으며, 델포이에서 살해되었다고 전해진다.

1) corner : 궁지로 몰다.

stag shall be quartered. The first quarter shall be mine, as I am the king of beasts."

"The second is mine, as this hunt was my idea."

"The third quarter is mine, for I led the chase."

"And the fourth quarter, sire?" asked the monkey.

The lion drew himself up and gave an ominous growl.

"As for the fourth quarter — let him take it who dares."

▶ ***Moral*** : Many may share in the labor but not in the spoils.

THE FOX AND THE GOAT

One day a fox fell into a deep well from which he could not escape. Just as he was about to give up hope, a goat came by to quench his thirst.

Seeing the fox in the well, the goat exclaimed, "What in the world are you doing in that well, old fox?"

"Haven't you heard news of the great drought? As soon as I heard, I jumped down here where the water is cool and plentiful. It is delicious too, and I have drunk so much I can hardly move."

When the goat heard this, he jumped into the well, and the fox immediately jumped onto the goat's back and up his horns, scrambling to safety.

▶ ***Moral*** : It is not safe to trust the advice of a man in difficulties.

THE MONKEY AND THE CAMEL

The monkey was a great and nimble entertainer. At a grand gathering of all the beasts, the monkey danced and sang and told stories that made all the animals roar with laughter.

Only the camel seemed bored by the monkey's performances. "What a dull show you put on, little monkey," sniffed the camel. "It has almost put me to sleep."

"Can you do better?" asked the monkey.

"Of course I can," said the camel, shuffling onto the stage and doing a clumsy dance and singing an off-key[2)] song of the desert.

All the beasts booed her and set upon her with clubs and stones and drove the foolish camel out into the vast desert.

▶ ***Moral*** : Stretch your arm no longer than your sleeve.

THE ANT AND THE GRASSHOPPER

The grasshopper took his ease in the fields all summer long, chirping and singing, while his neighbor the ant plodded the dusty road carrying kernels of wheat to his nest. "What a stupid oaf[3)] to work in this heat,"

---

2) off-key : 음이 맞지 않는, 음정이 고르지 않은

3) oaf : 바보, 멍청이

thought the grasshopper. "Summer is the time for fun."

But when winter came with its icy blasts, the grasshopper was cold and hungry, and he came shivering to the ant's nest begging for food. "Help me, I am starving," cried the grasshopper.

"Are you not the same grasshopper who was lazy and played in the fields all summer?" asked the ant.

"Yes, I am," said the grasshopper.

"Since you sang all summer," replied the ant, "you can dance all winter."

▶ ***Moral*** : Prepare for the days of necessity.

THE FOX AND THE CROW

The crow flew to the top of a tree to enjoy a piece of cheese she had stolen.

A wily fox spied the cheese in the crow's beak, and his mouth watered for it as he spoke these words : "O beautiful crow, charming crow, delightful crow, how wonderful to see you in all your glory!"

The crow smiled, holding the cheese firmly in her beak.

"You are the most exquisite of birds—and though I have not heard your voice, I am quite sure it must surpass that of any other bird."

The vain crow was pleased by all this flattery, especially the part about her voice, for she had sometimes been told that her caw was unpleasant.

She opened her beak to sing for the fox, and out fell the cheese into the fox's watering jaws.

▶ ***Moral*** : Beware of flattery.

THE LION AND THE THREE BULLS

From afar, a hungry lion observed three bulls grazing beside one another in the same pasture. He imagined they would make a hearty meal, but he was afraid to attack all three at the same time.

Instead, he ambled[4] closer and, displaying a friendly face, struck up a whispered conversation with the bulls, telling each one separately about a small spot where the grass was exceptionally sweet and tender. After advising them not to share this information, he watched as the bulls slipped away, to different sections of the field.

There, the lion ambushed them as they stood alone; then feasted on them one by one at his leisure.

▶ ***Moral*** : There is strength in numbers.

4) amble : 천천히 걷다.

THE ANGLER AND THE LITTLE FISH

All day long the angler[5] fished without a single bite. Just as he was about to call it a day[6], there was a small tug[7] at his line and he pulled in a tiny perch.

"O please spare me, fisherman," cried the perch. "I am so small, I am hardly a mouthful. But I do have an idea. Throw me back into the river and let me grow big and plump enough to make you a tasty meal. Then come back and I'll let you catch me again, and we'll all be happy."

The fisherman thought a moment and then shook his head. "No, no," he said, "I have you in hand now, but once you get back into the water your tune will be, 'Catch me if you can!'"

▶ ***Moral*** : Beware the promises of a desperate man.

THE PORCUPINE AND THE SNAKES

One cold, wet day, a porcupine was searching for shelter from the pouring rain. Finally, she found a den of snakes, who invited her in.

"Snakes!" she shuddered. But she was desperate, and as the snakes

---

5) angler : 낚시꾼
6) call it a day : (오늘은) 그만해 두다, 일을 그만두다, 단념하다
7) tug : 여기서는 '입질'의 의미임.

seemed mild and amiable, she entered and began to feel quite at home.

The snakes, on the other hand, found that their guest's presence created remarkable discomfort. No matter how they twisted and coiled, there was another quill,[8] waiting to poke them!

"We're sorry, but we must ask you to leave now," they said.

But the porcupine liked being warm and dry.

"I, myself, intend to stay," she replied. "You may go, or stay if you choose. It's all the same to me."

▶ ***Moral*** : Temper[9] generosity with wisdom.

THE RAVEN AND THE SWAN

A raven saw a swan and envied the other bird's beautiful white plumage.

"Perhaps it's because he spends so much time in the water," mused the raven, supposing he might wash his own feathers clean and achieve the dazzling hue he admired.

With this aim in mind, he traded his customary haunts for the swan's lakes and streams. But his constant bathing failed to transform his feathers, and at last, grown thin and weak from lack of food, he died.

---

8) quill : 호저의 가시

9) temper : 조화시키다, 조절하다

▶ ***Moral*** : A change of habit won't alter Nature.

THE BUNDLE OF STICKS

Once there was a farmer with many sons, who were always fighting and quarreling among themselves. One day he called his sons together. Before him lay a bundle of sticks tied together.

He commanded each son to take up the bundle of sticks and break it in two. Each son tried and each one failed. Then the father untied the bundle and gave them the sticks to break one by one. They did this with ease.

"My sons," said the father, "by this example you can see that there is strength in being together. But once you quarrel and are separated, you are easily destroyed."

▶ ***Moral*** : In unity there is strength.

THE WOLF IN SHEEP'S CLOTHING

A fierce wolf had been stalking a flock of sheep for many days, but the shepherd had been so vigilant[10] in guarding his animals that the wolf had been unable to catch one.

---

10) vigilant : 방심하지 않는, 끊임없이 경계하는

"I shall disguise myself," said the wolf. He wrapped himself in a sheep-skin and made his way among the grazing sheep. "Baa, baa," said the wolf, deceiving both the shepherd and his sheep.

When night came, the shepherd led his flock of sheep, including one wolf in sheep's clothing, into the fold.

Later that evening the shepherd wanted something for his supper. He went down to the fold and seized the first animal he came upon. It was the wolf in sheep's clothing, and the shepherd feasted on wolf that night.

▶ ***Moral*** : Every deceit has its dangers.

THE TORTOISE AND THE HARE

The hare was very proud of his fleetness of foot and enjoyed teasing the tortoise for being so slow and plodding. At last the tortoise could not abide the teasing any longer, and he challenged the hare to a foot race.

"You challenge me to a race?" said the hare. "That is ridiculous!"

"Enough talk," snapped the tortoise. "Let the race begin."

The course was set by the animals, and the fox was chosen as judge. He gave a sharp bark and the race was begun. In a flash the hare was out of sight, far ahead of the plodding tortoise.

"Ho hum," yawned the hare, "I have time to take a nap and still beat that slowpoke[11)]." So he stretched himself out on a grassy knoll and snoozed in the afternoon sun.

Onward plodded the tortoise. He plodded beyond the sleeping hare. He plodded over the finish line! The hare woke up with a start to realize the race was lost.

▶ ***Moral*** : Slow and steady wins the race.

---

11) slowpoke : 느림보, 굼벵이

Be in Shape to Drive*

Driving safely is not always easy. In fact, it is one of the most complex things that people do. It also is one of the few things we do regularly that can injure and kill us. It is worth the effort to be a careful driver.

To be a safe driver, it takes a lot of skill and judgement. This task is even more difficult when you are just learning to drive. Driving can easily take all the ability you have. If anything happens so you are not up to your ability, you may not be a safe driver. Your ability to be a safe driver depends on being able to see clearly, not being overly tired, not driving while on drugs, being generally healthy, and being emotionally fit to drive. In other words, being in "shape"[1] to drive safely.

* 미국 Montana주의 2005년 운전면허시험을 위한 교본(2005 Driver's License Manual)에서 발췌한 것임.

1) in shape : 건강하여, 몸의 컨디션이 좋아

VISION AND HEARING[2)]

VISION

Good vision is a must for safe driving. You drive based on what you see. If you cannot see clearly, you will have trouble identifying traffic and road conditions, spotting potential trouble, and reacting in a timely manner.

Vision is so important that Montana requires that you pass a vision test before you get a driver's license. This test measures that you have at least 20/40 vision in at least one eye, with or without corrective lenses.[3)]

Because it is so important for safe driving to see well, you should have your eyes checked every year or two by an eye specialist. You may never know you have poor vision unless your eyes are tested.

If you need to wear glasses or contact lenses for driving, remember to:

- Always wear them when you drive, even if it is only to run down to the corner.[4)] If your driver license says you must wear corrective lenses and you are not and you happen to be stopped, you could get a ticket.[5)]
- Try to keep an extra pair of glasses in your vehicle. Then if your reg-

---

2) vision and hearing : 시력 및 청력

3) 미국의 시력 검사표의 한 단위. 미국의 시력 검사표는 눈이 나쁜 순서부터 좋은 순서로 20/200, 20/100, 20/64, 20/50, 20/40, 20/32, 20/25, 20/20의 8단계로 구성되어 있다. 가장 좋은 20/20은 한국의 시력 검사표의 2.0에 해당한다.

4) run down to the corner : 길모퉁이까지 달리다. 여기서는 "아주 적은 거리를 이동하다"라는 의미임.

5) a ticket : (교통위반자에 대한) 호출장, 빨간 (위반) 딱지

ular glasses were to break or be lost, you can drive safely. This also can be helpful if you do not wear glasses all the time. It is easy to misplace them.

- Avoid using dark glasses or tinted contact lenses at night, even if it is help with glare. The problem is that they cut down too much light. Light that you need to see clearly.

Other important aspects of vision are :

Side Vision

You need to see "out the corner of your eye". This lets you spot vehicles and other potential trouble on either side of you while you look ahead. Because you cannot focus on things to the side, you also must use your side mirrors and glance to the side if necessary.

Judging Distances And Speeds

Even if you can see clearly, you still may not be able to judge distances or speeds very well. In fact, you are not alone; many people have problems judging distances and speeds. It takes a lot of practice to be able to judge both. It is especially important in knowing how far you are from other vehicles and judging safe gaps when merging,[6] and when passing on two lane roads.

6) merge : (두 차선이) 합치다

Night Vision

Many people who can see clearly in the daytime have trouble seeing at night. All people have more trouble seeing at night than in the daytime. Some drivers have problems with glare[7] while driving at night, especially with the glare of oncoming headlights. If you have problems seeing at night, don't drive more than is necessary, and when you do, be very careful.

HEARING

Hearing can be helpful to safe driving. The sound of horns, a siren, or screeching tires can warn you of danger. Hearing problems, like bad eye-sight, can come on so slowly that you do not notice it. Drivers who know they are deaf or have hearing problems can adjust and be safe drivers. They learn to rely more on their vision and stay alert. Studies have shown that the driving records of hearing impaired drivers[8] are just as good as those drivers with good hearing.

FATIGUE

When you are tired, you cannot drive as safely as when you are rested. You do not see as well or are as alert as when you are rested. It takes

7) glare : (야간운전시의) 눈부신 빛, 번쩍이는 빛
8) hearing impaired driver : 청각 장애 운전자

you more time to make decisions and you do not always make good decisions.

You can be more irritable and can get upset more easily. Lastly, when you are tired, you could fall asleep behind the wheel and crash. The following are things you can do to help from getting tired on a long trip.

- Try to get a normal night's sleep before you leave.
- Do not leave on a trip if you are already tired. Plan your trips so you can leave when you are rested.
- Eat lightly. Do not eat a large meal before you leave. Some people get sleepy after they eat a big meal.
- Take breaks. Stop every two hours or so, or when you need to. Walk around, get some fresh air, and have some coffee, soda, or juice. The few minutes spent on a rest break can save your life.
- Plan for plenty of time to complete your trip safely.
- Try not to drive late at night when you are normally asleep. Your body thinks it is time to go to sleep and will try to do so.
- Never drive if you are sleepy. It is better to stop and sleep for a few hours than to take a chance you can stay awake. If possible switch off with another driver[9] and you can sleep while they drive.

9) switch off with another driver : 다른 운전자와 교대하다.

DRINKING AND DRIVING

Alcohol is involved in about 40% of the traffic accidents in which somebody is killed. If you drink alcohol, even a little, your chances of being in an accident are much greater than if you did not drink any alcohol.

No one can drink alcohol and drive safely, even if you have been driving for many years. New drivers are more affected by alcohol than experienced drivers, because new drivers are still learning to drive.

Because drinking alcohol and then driving is dangerous, the penalties are very tough. People who drive after drinking risk getting heavy fines,[10)] higher insurance rates, loss of license, and even jail sentences.

WHY IS DRINKING AND DRIVING SO DANGEROUS?

Alcohol reduces all of the important skill you need to drive safely. After you drink alcohol, it goes from your stomach into your blood and to all parts of your body. It reaches your brain in 20 to 40 minutes. In your brain, alcohol affects those areas of your brain that controls judgement and skill. This is one reason why drinking alcohol is so dangerous—it affects your judgement. Good judgement is important to driving. But in this case, judgement helps you to know when to stop drinking. In a way, it's like alcohol puts good judgement on hold. You do not know when you have

10) fine : (n.) 벌금

had too much to drink until it is too late. It is a little like a sunburn — by the time you feel it, it is already too late.

Alcohol slows your reflexes[11)] and reaction time, reduces your ability to see clearly, and makes you less alert. As the amount of alcohol in your body increases, your judgement worsens and your skill decreases. You will have trouble judging distances, speeds and the movement of other vehicles. Finally, you will have trouble controlling your vehicle.

IF YOU DRINK, WHEN CAN YOU DRIVE?

The best advice is: If you drink alcohol, do not drive. Even one drink of alcohol can affect your driving.

An alcohol drink is a 1 ~ 1/2 oz. of 80-proof liquor(one shot glass), straight or with a mixer, 12 ounces of beer (a regular size can, bottle, mug or glass), or a 5 oz. glass of wine. Specialty drinks can have more alcohol in them and are the same as having several normal drinks.

It takes about an hour for your body to get rid of each drink. So, even if you have spread out your drinks, you should stop drinking at least one hour before you have to drive. There is no way to sober up quickly. Coffee, fresh air, exercise or cold showers will not help. Sleep will not help you to sober up.

Time is the only thing that will sober you up.

---

11) reflex : 반사작용

There are ways of dealing with social drinking situations. Arrange to go with two or more persons, where one of you will not drink alcohol. You can rotate among the group being a "designated driver". If available, you might use public transportation or use a cab.

If you drink alcohol, there are ways to control the effects. The best is to space out[12] your drinking. If you drink 1 drink an hour alcohol will not build up in your blood and you will not be affected. Another is to eat before and while you are drinking. Food in your stomach slows down how fast alcohol gets into your blood. Starchy foods like potato chips, pretzels, bread and crackers are best. But remember, food only slows when alcohol gets in your blood, it will not keep you from getting drunk.

ALCOHOL AND THE LAW

You are not allowed to buy alcohol unless you are 21 years of age.

If you are arrested for drinking and driving, the penalties are severe. You can be arrested for driving with a blood alcohol content(BAC)[13] of 0.08% or more, or while driving under the influence. BAC is the percentage of alcohol in your blood, and is usually determined by a breath, blood, or urine test.

If police officer asks you to take a test, you must do so. You can lose

12) space out : 시간차를 두다. 간격을 두다.

13) blood alcohol content : 혈중 알코올 농도

your driver license if you refuse to take a BAC test. If you are found guilty of an alcohol violation and it is your first conviction, you will be fined from $300 to $1000, plus court charges, you could be sentenced to 1 to 60 days in jail, and your license will be suspended for 6 months.

For second and subsequent convictions, the penalties are much worse.

Open Containers

Montana law also prohibits the possession of an open alcoholic beverage container by a person in a motor vehicle.

- Open alcoholic beverage containers, including bottles, cans, jars or other receptacles containing any amount of an alcoholic beverage must be kept:
  - In a locked glove compartment or storage compartment;
  - In a trunk, luggage compartment, truck bed or cargo compartment; or
  - Behind the last upright seat or within a closed container kept in an area not normally occupied by the driver or passenger of any motor vehicle that is not equipped with a trunk.

There are exceptions within the law for:

- Containers with an unbroken seal and none of the original contents removed;

- Open containers stored within the living quarters of a camper, travel trailer or motor home; and
- Passengers transported by a hired driver within a bus, taxi, or limousine.

But remember, it is an offense to unlawfully possess an open alcoholic beverage container within the passenger area of motor vehicle on a highway.

REPORT A DRUNK DRIVER

In December of 1981, the Governor, the Attorney General, and officials from the Montana Highway Traffic Safety Division, the Alcohol and Drug Abuse Division and the Montana Highway Patrol inaugurated the "Report A Drunk Driver" program. Nationally over 23,000 deaths occur yearly as a direct result of a drinking or drunk driver. In Montana, 50% of all traffic fatalities[14)] are alcohol related, and over 2100 injuries are the result of a drinking or drunk driver. The problem is immense and the "Report A Drunk Driver" program is designated to help rid the road and highways of your NUMBER ONE killer.

The program is very simple. All it requires is everyone's concern and a phone call. All citizens who suspect a person of driving while in-

14) fatalities : (pl.) 사망자(수)

toxicated are asked to call their local law enforcement agency or the Montana Highway Patrol and give a description in which the suspected vehicle was traveling. You do not have to give your name. Law enforcement personnel will attempt to make contact with the suspect vehicle and if probable cause can be determined, an arrest will be made.

The program works. Current statistics show that law enforcement officials are able to make contact with 37% of those suspected of driving under the influence, and of those contacted, 71% are being arrested for drunk driving. Two drinking drivers are being arrested each day in Montana as a direct result of this program. If you see someone you suspect of driving while intoxicated, or need to report an accident, you may call toll free 1-800-525-5555.

REPORT A DRUNK DRIVER
1-800-525-5555

OTHER DRUGS AND DRIVING

Besides alcohol, there are many other drugs that can affect a person's ability to drive safely. These drugs can have effects like those of alcohol, or even worse. This is true of many prescription drugs or even many of the drugs you can buy without a prescription. Drugs taken for headaches, colds, hay fever or other allergies, or to calm nerves can make a person drowsy and affect their driving. Pep pill,[15] "uppers",[16] and diet pills can make a driver feel more alert for a short time. Later, however, they can cause a person to be nervous, dizzy, not able to concentrate, and they can affect your vision. Other prescription drugs can affect your reflexes, judgement, vision, and alertness in way similar to alcohol.

If you are driving, check the label before you take a drug for warnings about its effects. If you are not sure if it is safe to take the drug and drive, ask your doctor or pharmacist about any side effects[17]. Never drink alcohol while you are taking other drugs. The drugs could multiply the effects of alcohol, or have additional side effects of their own. These effects not only reduce your ability to be a safe driver, but the effects could cause serious health problems, even death.

Illegal drugs are not good for your health and effect your ability to be a safe driver. For example, studies have shown that people who use marijuana make more mistakes, have more trouble adjusting to glare, and get arrested for traffic violations more than other drivers.

HEALTH

Many health problems can affect your driving — a bad cold, infection, or a virus. Even little problems like a stiff neck, a cough, or a sore leg

15) pep pill : 각성제
16) upper : 각성제
17) side effect : 부작용

can affect your driving. If you are not feeling well and need to go somewhere, let someone else drive. You should decide each time you drive, if you are physically able or mentally capable to drive safely.

Some health conditions can be very dangerous:

EPILEPSY[18)]

A person suffering from a condition needs a physician to attest in writing that the person's condition has stabilized and would not be likely to interfere with that person's ability to operate a motor vehicle safely.

DIABETES

Diabetics who take insulin should not drive when there is any chance of going into shock. Such a situation could result from skipping a meal or snack, or from taking the wrong amount of insulin. It also might be a good idea to have someone else drive during times when your doctor is adjusting your insulin dosage. If you have diabetes, you also should have your eyes checked regularly for possible night blindness and other vision problems.

HEART CONDITION

People with heart diseases, high blood pressure, or circulation problems and are in danger of a blackout, fainting, or a heart attack should not get

---

18) epilepsy : 간질, a fit of epilepsy : 간질 발작

behind the wheel. If a doctor is treating for you for a heart condition is ask if the condition could affect your driving safely.

EMOTIONS

Stress can lessen your concentration on the driving task and emotions can have a great affect on your driving safely. You may not be able to drive well if you are overly worried, excited, afraid, angry, or just down.

If you are angry or excited, give yourself time to cool off. If necessary, take a short walk, but stay off the road until you have calmed down. If you are worried or down about something, try to keep your mind on your driving. Some find listening to the radio helps. If you are impatient, give yourself extra time for your driving trip. Leave a few minutes early. If you have plenty of time, you may not tend to speed, or do other things that can get you a traffic ticket or cause a crash.

The Invisible Lover*

THE STORY OF Cupid AND Psyche TOLD BY APULEIUS

Once upon a time a king and queen had three very beautiful daughters, but much the most beautiful was the youngest, Psyche. People came from many lands to admire her, in the belief that she was Venus, or had succeeded her as goddess of love. This caused the rites of Venus to be neglected, and the goddess angrily bade her son Cupid wound Psyche so as to make her fall in love with some completely degraded creature. Venus then went on her way across the sea to her sacred island of Cyprus. But Psyche received no benefit from all the honours paid to her. Her sisters had married kings, yet no one courted Psyche, and she sat

* Apuleius의 *Cupid and Psyche*의 신화. Lucius Apuleius(A. D. 124?~A. D. 180?)는 아프리카 태생의 로마 작가로 작품에 라틴 소설 『황금의 당나귀』, 저서에 『변명(辨明)』 등이 있다.

alone at home, feeling ill and miserable.

Her father, suspecting divine anger, inquired from the oracle of Apollo at Miletus where he might find a husband for her. The answer, however, came that Psyche's husband was no human being but a winged serpent of whom even Jupiter was afraid ; she must put on black mourning and go to a mountain-top for her deathly marriage. To the accompaniment of funeral music and lamentation, she headed the procession like a woman going to her grave.

Sending away her parents, who shut themselves in their palace to grieve, Psyche climbed to the very top of the hill. A breeze came, and lifted her off the ground, and carried her down to a valley beneath, where she found herself laid upon a bed of flowery grass. After sleeping for a while there, she rose and walked beside a stream into the depths of a wood, and she came upon a palace so radiant with gold and gems and precious woods that she knew it was a god's. When she finally ventured to cross the threshold of this heavenly abode,[1] Psyche found within its doors unbelievably valuable treasures, with no guard to watch over them.

But the voice of an unseen maidservant guided her to her bedroom and bathroom. First she found her bedroom and dozed off again for a while, then she went to the bath, where invisible hands undressed her, washed her, anointed her and dressed her again in her bridal costume. As she wandered out of the bathroom she noticed a semi-circular table with a com-

1) abode : 거처, 주소, 체류

fortable chair in front of it; it was laid for a banquet, though there was nothing yet on it to eat or drink. She sat down expectantly—and at once nectarous[2] wines and appetizing dishes appeared by magic, floating up to her of their own accord. She saw nobody at all, the waiters were mere voices, and when someone came in and sang and someone else accompanied him on the lyre, she saw neither of them, nor the lyre either. Then a whole invisible choir burst into song.

When this delightful banquet was over, Psyche thought it must be about time to go to bed, so she went to her bedroom again and undressed and lay awake for a long time. Towards midnight she heard a gentle whispering near her, and began to feel lonely and scared. Anything might happen in a vast uninhabited place like this, and she had fears for her chastity. But no, it was the whisper of her unknown husband. He came and lay with her, without being seen, and left before daybreak; and the next two nights he visited her again. Meanwhile Psyche's parents, joined by her sisters, were still lamenting her as lost, but her unseen husband warned her not to answer her sisters if she heard them mourning. When, however, she pleaded to be allowed their company, he reluctantly relented,[3] but on the condition that she must not, however much they importuned her, try to find out what he looked like. So the West Wind brought her sisters to the palace, and Psyche, drawing upon her imagination, told them her husband

2) nectarous : 과즙의, 감미로운

3) relent : 상냥스러워지다, 약해지다, 누그러지다

was a handsome young man with his first beard, who liked hunting.

When they were alone with one another on their way back to their father's house, the elder sisters indulged in jealousy. One of them complained that her own husband was bald, feeble and miserly. The other grumbled that she was married to a man who suffered so badly from sciatica[4] and gout[5] that his wife was no more than a nurse, whose hands were ruined by his plasters[6] and poultices.[7] So they returned to their homes, full of malicious intentions; and now Psyche's husband again warned her of the danger from them, this time with the assurance that she was to have a baby by him—a god if she kept his secret, but only a mortal if she talked.

But next time she saw her sisters, Psyche was not sufficiently on her guard. She was very simple-minded and, forgetting what story she had told them before, invented a new one. She said that he was a middle-aged merchant from the next province, very rich, with slightly grizzled hair. Then, breaking the conversation off short, she loaded them with valuable presents and sent them away. As they rode home, the younger sister said: "Now, what do you make of the monstrous lies she tells us? First the silly creature says that her husband is a very young man with a downy beard, and then she says that he's middle-aged with grizzled hair! Quick work, eh?

4) sciatica : 좌골 신경통, 좌골통
5) gout : 통풍(痛風), 웅혈
6) plaster : 고약, 경고(硬膏)
7) poultice : 찜질약, 습포

You may depend upon it that the beast is either hiding something from us, or else she doesn't know herself what her husband looks like." "Whatever the truth may be," said the elder sister, "we must ruin her as soon as possible."

And so, correctly guessing the unwelcome prospect that Psyche's baby was destined to be a god, they deliberately frightened her by suggesting that her husband was a fiendish reptile. Accordingly, at their proposal, next time she was in bed with him she got up and took a lamp, and took also a carving knife to kill him. But by the light she saw he was Cupid himself in all his glory. She tried the point of one of his arrows, which pricked her, and the lamp she was carrying spilt a drop of burning oil upon his shoulder. He woke, and immediately departed from her, and flew to the top of a cypress-tree. After pausing there with a reproachful message, he soared up into the air and was gone.

After vainly trying to down herself—the river set her ashore—Psyche wandered off in aimless misery, and came to the city where one of her elder sisters lived. She told this woman what had happened, but deceitfully added: "As he flew away, he said that he would have you in my place as his wife." So, like Psyche before her, "the sister jumped off the rock too, shouting confidently: 'Here I come, Cupid, a woman worthy of your love. West Wind, convey your mistress to the Palace at once'." Then she took a head-long leap; but she never reached the valley, either dead or alive, because the rocks cut her to pieces as she fell and scattered her flesh and guts all over the mountain-side. So she got what she deserved, and the birds and beasts feasted on her remains. Soon afterwards the other sister met with the same fate.

Meanwhile, in his mother's celestial house, Cupid lay groaning with pain. Venus, who was bathing in the sea, was told of his affair by a sea-gull, and furiously complained to her stepmother Juno and Ceres about what had happened; but they, in fear of cupid's arrows, tried to excuse him. Psyche, looking everywhere for her lover, came to their shrines for protection. But although they would have liked to help her, they dared not offend Venus. After announcing a reward for anyone who could find Psyche, Venus — through her servant Custom — soon tracked her down. After two of her other women, Anxiety and Sadness, had whipped the girl, the goddess leapt on her, tore her clothes to rags, pulled out handfuls of her hair, and shook her repeatedly.

Then she imposed a series of formidable tasks. First, before nightfall, Psyche must sort out an enormous heap of wheat, barley, millet, lentils, beans and the seeds of poppy and vetch. "You look such a dreadful sight, slave," said Venus, "that the only way that you are ever likely to get a lover is by hard work"—and she flew off to a wedding-party, from which she returned at midnight, scented and slightly drunk. But Psyche, helped by an army of ants, had completed her task. She was then set a second and more dreadful task, of bringing Venus a piece of wool from some fiercely dangerous golden sheep on the bank of a stream. But this too, with the help of a green reed, she was able to achieve, and she brought Venus back a whole lap-full[8] of the golden wool.

Yet even her performance of this second perilous task did not satisfy the goddess, who frowned and told her with a cruel smile: "Someone has been helping you again, that's quite clear. But now I'll put your courage and prudence to a still severer test. Do you see the summit of that high mountain over there? You'll find that a dark-coloured stream cascades down its precipitous sides into a gorge below and then floods the Stygian marshes and feeds the hoarse River of Wailing. Here is a little jar. Go off at once and bring it back to me brimful of ice-cold water fetched from the very middle of the cascade where it bursts out of the rock." Psyche was horrified by the fierce dragons guarding the stream, but Providence came to her aid and sent her Jupiter's eagle, which owed Cupid a debt of gratitude for helping him carry Ganymede to heaven to be Jupiter's cup-bearer. With critical words for Psyche's silly simplicity, the eagle took the jar and induced the stream to give up its water.

Declaring Psyche was a witch, Venus now bade her take a box down to the Underworld itself, and hand it to Proserpina, with the request that the queen should put a little of her beauty inside the box, and send it back for Venus, who had expended some of her own beauty in looking after her sick son, and needed further supplies for a theatre-party that evening. Psyche was now desperate, and went up a high tower, resolved to throw herself from its top and reach the Underworld by killing herself. But the tower broke into speech, and dissuaded her. "Listen to me. The famous

8) lap-full : 앞치마 그득한 분량

Greek city of Lacedaemon(Sparta) is not far from here. Go there at once and ask to be directed to Taenarus, which is rather an out-of-the-way place to find. It's on a peninsula to the south. Once you get there you'll find one of the ventilation holes of the Underworld. Put your head through it and you'll see a road running down hill, but there'll be no traffic on it. Climb through at once and the road will lead you straight to Pluto's palace. But don't forget to take with you two pieces of barley-bread soaked in honey water, one in each hand, and two coins in your mouth.

"When you have gone a good way along the road you'll meet a lame ass loaded with wood, and its lame driver will ask you to hand him some pieces of rope for tying up part of the load which the ass has dropped. Pass him by in silence. Then hurry forward until you reach the river of the dead, where Charon will at once ask you for his fee and ferry you across in his patched boat among crowds of ghosts. It seems that the God Avarice lives thereabouts,[9] because neither Charon nor his great father Pluto does anything for nothing. (A poor man on the point of death is expected to have his passage-fee ready; but if he can't get hold of a coin, he isn't allowed to achieve true death, but must wander about disconsolately for ever on this side of Styx.) Anyhow, give the dirty ruffian one of your coins, but let him take it from your mouth not from your hand.

"While you are being ferried across the sluggish stream, the corpse of

---

9) thereabouts : 그 근처에, 그 부근에

an old man will float by. He will raise a putrid hand and beg you to haul him into the boat. But you must be careful not to yield to any feeling of pity for him; that is forbidden. Once ashore, you will meet three women some distance away from the bank. They will be weaving cloth and will ask you to help them. To touch the cloth is also forbidden. All these apparitions, and others like them, are snares set for you by Venus; her object is to make you let go one of the sops you are carrying, and you must understand that the loss of even one of them would be fatal — it would prevent your return to this world. They are for you to give to Cerberus, the huge, fierce, formidable hound with three heads on three necks, all barking in unison, who terrifies the dead; though of course the dead have no need to be frightened by him because they are only shadows and he can't injure shadows." After dealing with Cerberus, Psyche would be welcomed by Proserpina. But on her way back she must take care not to open or even look at the box. Its treasure was not for her.

All went well upon her dangerous quest, and she obeyed every instruction, until she was on her return journey and had left the Underworld behind. But then, out of a foolish desire to have some of the beauty for herself, she opened the box; and at once she fell down in a fatal sleep, as if she were dead.

But Cupid, now recovered, came to rouse and rescue her, and Psyche was able to rise to her feet and deliver Proserpina's present to Venus. Meanwhile her lover pleaded with Jupiter, who summoned the gods and goddesses to Council and told them Cupid had best stop roving and settle down with Psyche. Assuring Venus that this would be no disgrace for herself, he sent Mercury to bring Psyche up to heaven, and gave her a cup of nectar to make her immortal, and to keep Cupid, for all time, from flying away from her again.

Then Jupiter ordered a great wedding-banquet, at which, to the accompaniment of flute and pipe-music, the Muses chanted the marriage-hymn, and Apollo sang to his own lyre. And, as he sang, Venus performed a lively dance.

So Cupid and Psyche were married; and their child was a daughter called Pleasure.

TECHNOLOGY: Unwanted Master of the Universe

Don Coon

Financial Waste and Inequities

"Getting schools to leap onto the information Highway is just the latest in a series of corporate forays[1)] marked by ignorance, self-interest, and marketing madness." Despite a few promising experiments, there is no evidence that technology significantly alters school

1) forays: 시도

effectiveness. Business is behind this new spearhead for technology. They see the education 'market' as a great test bed for future technologies such as interactive TV. Why schools haven't learned from history is a mystery. Back in the 1960's there was a big movement to include modern technology into the schools. The companies that invested heavily in this 'market' went under[2]. The latest fad, wiring to the internet, is estimated to come in at $10 billion. Current trends have education subservient to technology instead of the other way around[3]. Technology should be education's servant but since big business is driving this wave of purchases, it is not turning out that way. "High-tech corporate moguls[4] and marketers, despite their government supporters are scrambling to predict the future, are seduced by their own high-tech fantasies, and are locked in treacherous high-stakes gambles". Even if this 'gamble' pays off[5], the distribution of these technologies is not equitable so the rewards will not be the same for all people.

Small rural school districts do not have the funds to keep up with technology. Often their tax base is shrinking as people move away. The traditional ways of life, found in rural areas, often minimizes the importance of technology. The lack of funds and incentive, coupled with the lack of technology training for teachers creates inequities regarding com-

---

2) went under: 망했다, 파산했다, 도산했다
3) the other way around: 반대로, 거꾸로
4) moguls: 거물
5) pays off: 좋은 결과를 얻다, 성공하다

puter use between metropolitan and rural schools. Equitable home use of computers is another source of concern. 82 percent of high-income 11th graders have home computers compared to 48 percent in middle-income homes and 14 percent in the low-income 11th graders' homes. How will low-income students keep up with the others in computer skills with only the limited exposure they can acquire in schools?

Culture Trampled on *The Oregon Trail*

Is technology riding roughshod over[6] various cultures, stripping them of their identities? Many believe this is so. Television is often vilified in this regard. Does educational technology have the same effect? According to Bill Bigelow, even some of the 'best' software, such as *Oregon Trail*, can reduce students perspective to that of white males. Though this software has received rave reviews on its "multicultural and gender-fair" perspectives, on closer inspection[7], it becomes apparent that perspectives, other than the white males', are only superficially addressed. "*Oregon Trail* is sexist, racist, culturally insensitive, and contemptuous of the earth. It imparts bad values and wrong history." Technology is created by programmers, who's cultural bias infects their work. To make this point, several examples will be sited with this 'five star' software.

---

6) riding roughshod over ~ : ~를 짓밟는 것, 함부로 대하는 것

7) on closer inspection: 좀 더 면밀히 관찰해보면

How does Oregon Trail portray women, African-Americans, Indians and environmental values? The learner is allowed to pick a profession, but not a gender or a race. They are immediately funneled into the white male perspective. Women are present in the simulation but their importance is minimized. Historically, they had as much responsibilities as the men, but this is not evident in the game. Blacks are present, but they are also marginalized[8]. In no way, do they represent what blacks of that time experienced. During that time, they were either slaves or servants with only the occasional emancipated black person on the trail. Laws in Oregon, barred blacks from owning land. The software's treatment of Indians, at first glance, seems enlightened but this is not the case.

Though the native Americans were never depicted as the enemy, their perspective was never shown. Conversations, from the software's characters, appear to respect the native populations perspective. Unfortunately, these conversations never recognize how inconsiderate the pioneers were with the Indian's resources. Pioneers, known as the 'Greedy People' by the Lakotas[9], stripped the area of much needed forest and game. Instead of paying for their impositions, pioneers fought the tribes whose lands they ruined. Nowhere in the simulation, is the disposition of the Oregon Indians indicated. This program never really addresses the conflicts between the settlers and the native Americans. After hours of play, the simulation gives

8) marginalized: 소외되다, 무시되다
9) Lakotas: 북아메리카 인디언 부족 중의 하나.

the impression that the learner, now totally immersed in the pioneer's white male perspective, is entitled to the promise land—no matter who else gets displaced. If a "multicultural and gender-fair" software package, as *Oregon Trail* claims to be, is written with such bias, how do the other technologies stack up?

Class: Master or Slave?

Computers have been touted[10] as the great equalizers. If all schools have the same computer access, wouldn't it follow that all learners are getting the same experience? The research does not bear this out. Computers get used in quite different ways in higher-income settings than in the low-income locales. Drill and Practice software is over-represented in the low-income schools while much more creative and liberating uses are devised in the more affluent neighborhoods. Research has shown that computers should help the student construct their knowledge for the best learning result—be the students servant. Students word process, research on the web, create web pages, graphics, and multimedia presentations for a very rich educational experience. Drill and practice software, on the other hand, is the master and the student must obediently follow it. The computer teaches and then requires responses from the student before proceeding. This approach stifles learning. Educators defend this by saying that the

10) touted: 지나치게 칭찬을 받았다, 사도록 권유되었다, 강매되었다

low-income student are not ready for higher-order thinking. Perhaps these teachers, from lack of confidence with the technology or lack of faith in the students, are more comfortable with the 'canned' teaching programs. The net outcome is that, instead of all students progressing from technologies influence, the gap is widening in technological prowess between the economic class boundaries.

Doomsday Warrior kills Female Gender

With the gap between the classes increasing on the technological front, is there also a disparity between the sexes? Boys and girls show the same tendencies regarding computers until their early teens and then boys pull ahead with technology. In college, there are far fewer females in computer classes. Perhaps stereotypes are being reinforced, where teachers, parents, and peers alike assume that boys are naturally better at technology. Perhaps the logic utilized in the computer is more suited for males since the machines, for the most part, are designed by men, programmed by men, and originally created for military purposes. This same trend is evident in the computer gaming business where most games are purchased for boys.

Many computer games are very militaristic with names like "Pit-Fighter, Final Fight, Blades of Vengeance, and Doomsday Warrior." Girls do not like most of the available computer games — they represent 25% percent of the market. Is this just biological differences of the hunters and the gatherers which cannot be altered or is it the male software designers inability to find themes that work well for females?

Instructional designers have produced materials for public, private and military schools which continue to reinforce stereotypes as does their promotions and media messages which they play on television and other entertainment media. Stereotypes can be found everywhere in computer technology. Men are portrayed in authority positions while women are seen as subservient—these tendencies are everywhere from clip art to the programs themselves (as illustrated in *The Oregon Trail*). Computers, as a consequence, appear to be "male territory". This myth is spilling into all facets of education. It is evident in how boys are prepared for leadership positions, how male sport figures are worshiped, the way stereotypes are promoted in toy marketing strategies, and the disparity teachers demonstrate when responding to boys and girls. Since technology has, so pervasively, waved its male supremacy flag, should it be allowed to maintain and increase its presence in the educational community?

Closing Remarks on Technology's Negative Effects

Despite all the fanfare, computer technology has not made school life more equitable. The differences have enlarged. Those who are getting ahead are getting further ahead while those who were left behind are now way back on the horizon, soon to go out of sight. Technology is another 'nail in the coffin', one more issue that empowers the privileged at the expense of the rest of society. Technology is serving its producers only, big business, while enslaving education in America. Is it really necessary? Or perhaps, it is doing more harm than good.

The Battle Over Same-Sex Marriage

Bob Egelko

Gays and lesbians have no constitutional right to marry in California, and any change giving them that right must come from state lawmakers or the voters rather than the legal system, a state appeals court declared Thursday.

The 2-1 decision reversed a lower-court ruling[1] in favor of plaintiffs who were among the thousands of gays and lesbians who married at San Francisco City Hall in 2004. It cleared the way for both sides to argue their case before the state Supreme Court, which will have the final say

1) ruling: 판결, 판례

on whether the courts can give same-sex couples the right to marry.

San Francisco Superior Court Richard Kramer ruled last year that a 1977 state law defining marriage as a union between a man and a woman violated the state Constitution by denying gays and lesbians the right to marry the partners of their choice. Kramer also found that the law discriminated on the basis of sex.

By contrast, the ruling Thursday by the First District Court of Appeal in San Francisco focused on the law's roots in the traditional definition of marriage, the prerogatives of state legislators and voters to make social policy and the limits of judicial authority.

The central issue is "who gets to define marriage in our democratic society," Presiding Justice William McGuiness said in the majority opinion, which was joined by Justice Joanne Parrilli. "We believe this power rests in the people and their elected representatives."

He said there were major differences between this case and the California Supreme Court's landmark 1948 ruling that struck down[2] the state's ban on interracial marriage. That ruling did not purport to change the traditional definition of marriage, McGuiness said. Instead, it took aim at the law's perpetuation of racial discrimination, which — unlike discrimination based on sexual orientation — is condemned in the U.S. Constitution, McGuiness said.

"We believe it is rational for the Legislature to preserve the opposite-sex

2) struck down: 무효로 만들었다.

definition of marriage, which has existed throughout history and which continues to represent the common understanding of marriage in most other countries and states of our union," McGuinness said.

He also pointed to recent steps by the state, giving registered domestic partners the same rights as spouses under California law, as evidence that the state is not discriminating against same-sex couples. Those laws are not recognized by the federal government, however, and do not entitle same-sex partners to benefits in such areas as Social Security, income taxes and immigration.

McGuiness said the fundamental right to marry applied only to traditional opposite-sex unions.

"That such a right is irrelevant to a lesbian or gay person does not mean the definition of the fundamental right can be expanded by the judicial branch beyond its traditional moorings[3)]," he said.

Dissenting Justice J. Anthony Kline said the ruling condones[4)] the same kind of bias that the state's high court outlawed in 1948. He said the majority's conclusion that laws that discriminate against gays and lesbians are more tolerable than racist laws "requires us to deny as judges what we know as people."

Kline also said the definition of marriage accepted by the appeals court —excluding a class of people based on their sexual orientation—"demeans

3) moorings: 안전한 곳, 보호된 영역
4) condones: 묵인하다, 눈감아주다

the institution of marriage and diminishes the humanity of the gay men and lesbians who wish to marry a loved one of their choice."

Advocates of same-sex marriage joined Kline's criticism, saying the court had offered no rationale for the law other than a discriminatory tradition.

"If other courts had followed this line of reasoning, we would still have segregation," said San Francisco City Attorney Dennis Herrera, whose office joined groups of same-sex couples in suits challenging the marriage law.

But the tone of Thursday's ruling, deferring to the judgments of elected officials and voters and prescribing a modest role for the courts, could appeal to the state Supreme Court. The court has issued several pro-gay-rights rulings, including decisions last year upholding parental status for lesbian partners, but seldom overturns state laws or executive decisions.

"What's significant is the level of review" in McGuiness' ruling, said Mathew Staver, chairman of Liberty Counsel, a conservative organization that represented opponents of gay rights and same-sex marriage in the case.

In the appeals court's view, he noted, "it doesn't matter whether judges disagree with the policy. What matters is whether the Legislature has a rational and legitimate basis to restrict marriage to one man and one woman."

Shannon Minter, legal director of the National Center for Lesbian Rights and a lawyer for 12 same-sex couples in the case, said he was confident that the state's high court would at least subject the law to closer scrutiny.

Under Thursday's ruling, the fact that lesbians and gays have never been allowed to marry "is a reason enough to exclude them from marriage," Minter said. "We may lose (at the Supreme Court), but if we do, they won't rely on reasoning like that. I think we'll win."

The plaintiffs plan to file their appeals next month, and the Supreme Court would then have up to 90 days to decide whether to let Thursday's ruling stand or — as generally expected — accept the case for review. A hearing could take place in late 2007, with a ruling due 90 days later.

The high court already weighed in on[5] an aspect of the case in August 2004, when it overturned nearly 4,000 same-sex marriages performed at San Francisco City Hall in February and March of that year on the authority of Mayor Gavin Newsom. The court said Newsom had exceeded his authority by defying the marriage law, but it did not rule on the validity of the law.

While the case was pending, the Legislature passed a bill that would have legalized same-sex marriage. But Gov. Arnold Schwarzenegger vetoed it, saying voter approval was needed because of a 2000 ballot initiative reaffirming the 1977 marriage statute and denying recognition of same-sex marriages performed in other states. Schwarzenegger said the issue should be decided in the courts.

---

5) weighed in on: 의견을 내놓았다.

The Pleasure of Reading Poems

My Heart Leaps Up

William Wordsworth

My heart leaps up when I behold
    A rainbow in the sky:
So was it when my life began;
So is it now I am a man;
So be it[1] when I shall grow old,
    Or let me die!
The Child is father of the Man;
And I could wish my days to be
Bound each to each by natural piety[2].

1) So be it: It shall be so. 늙어서도 그럴 것이다.

The Lake Isle of Innisfree

William Butler Yeats

I will arise and go now, and go to Innisfree[1],
And a small cabin build there, of clay and wattles made:
Nine bean-rows will I have there, a hive for the honeybee,
And live alone in the bee-loud glade[2].

And I shall have some peace there, for peace comes dropping slow,
Dropping from the veils of the morning to where the cricket sings;
There midnight's all a glimmer, and noon a purple glow,
And evening full of the linnet's wings.

I will arise and go now, for always night and day
I hear lake water lapping with low sounds by the shore;
While I stand on the roadway, or on the pavements grey,
I hear it in the deep heart's core.

---

2) natural piety: piety to nature. 자연에 대한 경외

1) Innisfree: 예이츠가 어린 시절에 자주 갔던 외갓집이 있는 아일랜드 서부 Sligo근처의 Gill 호수 가운데 있는 작은 섬.

2) bee-loud glade: 벌이 붕붕대는 소리로 요란한 숲.

The Road Not Taken

Robert Frost

Two roads diverged in a yellow wood,
And sorry I could not travel both
And be one traveler[1], long I stood
And looked down one as far as I could
To where it bent in the undergrowth;

Then took the other, as just as fair,
And having perhaps the better claim[2],
Because it was grassy and wanted wear[3];
Though as for that the passing there
Had worn them really about the same,

And both that morning equally lay
In leaves no step had trodden black[4].
Oh, I kept the first for another day!
Yet knowing how way leads on to way,
I doubted if I should ever come back.

---

1) I could not travel both/ And be one traveler: 몸이 하나라 두 길을 다 갈 수가 없었다.
2) having perhaps the better claim: 더 나은 것 같았다.
3) wanted wear: 길이 덜 닳아 있었다.
4) had trodden black: 밟아서 더럽힌

I shall be telling this with a sigh
Somewhere ages and ages hence:
Two roads diverged in a wood, and I —
I took the one less traveled by,
And that has made all the difference.

The Story of Silent Spring

How a courageous woman took on the chemical industry and raised important questions about humankind's impact on nature.

Although their role will probably always be less celebrated than wars, marches, riots or stormy political campaigns, it is books that have at times most powerfully influenced social change in American life. Thomas Paine's *Common Sense* galvanized[1)] radical sentiment in the early days of the American revolution; *Uncle Tom's Cabin* by Harriet Beecher Stowe roused Northern antipathy to slavery in the decade leading up to the Civil War; and Rachel Carson's *Silent Spring*, which in 1962 exposed the hazards of the pesticide DDT, eloquently questioned humanity's faith in technological progress and helped set the stage for the environmental

1) galvanized: 자극했다, 활기를 불어넣었다.

movement.

Carson, a renowned nature author and a former marine biologist with the U.S. Fish and Wildlife Service, was uniquely equipped to create so startling and inflammatory a book. A native of rural Pennsylvania, she had grown up with an enthusiasm for nature matched only by her love of writing and poetry. The educational brochures she wrote for the Fish and Wildlife Service, as well as her published books and magazine articles, were characterized by meticulous research and a poetic evocation of her subject.

"Things Go Out of Kilter"[2]

Carson was happiest writing about[3] the strength and resilience[4] of natural systems. Her books *Under the Sea Wind, The Sea Around Us* (which stayed on the *New York Times* bestseller list for 86 weeks), and *The Edge of The Sea* were hymns to the inter-connectedness of nature and all living things. Although she rarely used the term, Carson held an ecological view of nature, describing in precise yet poetic language the complex web of life that linked mollusks to sea-birds to the fish swimming in the ocean's deepest and most inaccessible reaches.

DDT, the most powerful pesticide the world had ever known, exposed

---

2) out of kilter: 제대로 작동하지 않는, 상태가 나쁜

3) happiest writing about~: ~에 대해 글을 쓸 때 가장 행복했다.

4) resilience: 원상태로 돌아가는 힘, 복원력, 회복력

nature's vulnerability. Unlike most pesticides, whose effectiveness is limited to destroying one or two types of insects, DDT was capable of killing hundreds of different kinds at once. Developed in 1939, it first distinguished itself during World War II, clearing South Pacific islands of malaria-causing insects for U.S. troops, while in Europe being used as an effective de-lousing powder. Its inventor was awarded the Nobel Prize.

When DDT became available for civilian use in 1945, there were only a few people who expressed second thoughts[5)] about this new miracle compound. One was nature writer Edwin Way Teale, who warned, "A spray as indiscriminate as DDT can upset the economy of nature as much as a revolution upsets social economy. Ninety percent of all insects are good, and if they are killed, things go out of kilter right away." Another was Rachel Carson, who wrote to the *Reader's Digest* to propose an article about a series of tests on DDT being conducted not far from where she lived in Maryland. The magazine rejected the idea.

Silent Spring

Thirteen years later, in 1958, Carson's interest in writing about the dangers of DDT was rekindled when she received a letter from a friend in Massachusetts bemoaning the large bird kills which had occured on Cape Cod as the result of DDT sprayings. The use of DDT had proliferated

---

5) second thoughts: 재고, 다시 생각함, 의문을 가짐, 다른 생각.

greatly since 1945 and Carson again tried, unsuccessfully, to interest a magazine in assigning her the story of its less desirable effects. By 1958 Carson was a best-selling author, and the fact that she could not obtain a magazine assignment to write about DDT is indicative of how heretical and controversial her views on the subject must have seemed. Having already amassed a large quantity of research on the subject, however, Carson decided to go ahead and tackle the DDT issue in a book.

Silent Spring took Carson four years to complete. It meticulously described how DDT entered the food chain and accumulated in the fatty tissues of animals, including human beings, and caused cancer and genetic damage. A single application on a crop, she wrote, killed insects for weeks and months, and not only the targeted insects but countless more, and remained toxic in the environment even after it was diluted by rainwater. Carson concluded that DDT and other pesticides had irrevocably harmed birds and animals and had contaminated the entire world food supply. The book's most haunting and famous chapter, "A Fable for Tomorrow," depicted a nameless American town where all life—from fish to birds to apple blossoms to human children—had been "silenced" by the insidious effects of DDT.

First serialized in *The New Yorker* in June 1962, the book alarmed readers across America and, not surprisingly, brought a howl of indignation from the chemical industry. "If man were to faithfully follow the teachings of Miss Carson," complained an executive of the American Cyanamid Company, "we would return to the Dark Ages, and the insects and diseases and vermin would once again inherit the earth." Monsanto published and distributed 5,000 copies of a brochure parodying *Silent Spring* entitled "The Desolate Year," relating the devastation and inconvenience of a world where famine, disease, and insects ran amuck[6] because chemical pesticides had been banned. Some of the attacks were more personal, questioning Carson's integrity and even her sanity.

Vindication

Her careful preparation, however, had paid off[7]. Anticipating the reaction of the chemical industry, she had compiled *Silent Spring* as one would a lawyer's brief, with no fewer than 55 pages of notes and a list of experts who had read and approved the manuscript. Many eminent scientists rose to her defense, and when President John F. Kennedy ordered the President's Science Advisory Committee to examine the issues the book raised, its report thoroughly vindicated both *Silent Spring* and its author. As a result, DDT came under much closer government supervision and was eventually banned. The public debate moved quickly from *whether* pesticides were dangerous to *which* pesticides were dangerous, and the burden of proof shifted from the opponents of unrestrained pesticide use to the chemicals' manufacturers.

---

6) ran amuck: ran amok. 창궐하다, 만연하다, 마구 번지다.
7) paid off: 결실을 맺었다, 좋은 결과를 얻었다.

The most important legacy of *Silent Spring,* though, was a new public awareness that nature was vulnerable to human intervention. Rachel Carson had made a radical proposal: that, at times, technological progress is so fundamentally at odds with natural processes that it must be curtailed. Conservation had never raised much broad public interest, for few people really worried about the disappearance of wilderness. But the threats Carson had outlined—the contamination of the food chain, cancer, genetic damage, the deaths of entire species — were too frightening to ignore. For the first time, the need to regulate industry in order to protect the environment became widely accepted, and environmentalism was born.

Carson was well aware of the larger implications of her work. Appearing on a CBS documentary about *Silent Spring* shortly before her death from breast cancer in 1964, she remarked, "Man's attitude toward nature is today critically important simply because we have now acquired a fateful power to alter and destroy nature. But man is a part of nature, and his war against nature is inevitably a war against himself? We are challenged as mankind has never been challenged before to prove our maturity and our mastery, not of nature, but of ourselves."

One of the landmark books of the 20th century, *Silent Spring's* message resonates loudly today, even several decades after its publication. And equally inspiring is the example of Rachel Carson herself. Against overwhelming difficulties and adversity, but motivated by her unabashed love of nature, she rose like a gladiator in its defense.

Solitude

Henry David Toreau*

This is a delicious evening, when the whole body is one sense, and imbibes delight through every pore. I go and come with a strange liberty in Nature, a part of herself. As I walk along the stony shore of the pond in my shirt-sleeves, though it is cool as well as cloudy and windy, and I see nothing special to attract me, all the elements[1] are unusually congenial to me. The bullfrogs trump to usher in the night, and the note of the whip-poor-will is borne on the rippling wind from over the water. Sympathy with the fluttering alder and poplar leaves almost takes away my breath; yet, like the lake, my serenity is rippled but not ruffled. These

1) all the elements: 날씨, (특히) 궂은 날씨, 비 · 바람 등

small waves raised by the evening wind are as remote from storm as the smooth reflecting surface. Though it is now dark, the wind still blows and roars in the wood, the waves still dash, and some creatures lull the rest with their notes. The repose is never complete. The wildest animals do not repose, but seek their prey now; the fox, and skunk, and rabbit, now roam the fields and woods without fear. They are Nature's watchmen — links which connect the days of animated life.

When I return to my house I find that visitors have been there and left their cards, either a bunch of flowers, or a wreath of evergreen, or a name in pencil on a yellow walnut leaf or a chip. They who come rarely to the woods take some little piece of the forest into their hands to play with by the way, which they leave, either intentionally or accidentally. One has peeled a willow wand, woven it into a ring, and dropped it on my table. I could always tell if visitors had called in my absence, either by the bended twigs or grass, or the print of their shoes, and generally of what sex or age or quality they were by some slight trace left, as a flower dropped, or a bunch of grass plucked and thrown away, even as far off as the railroad, half a mile distant, or by the lingering odor of a cigar or pipe. Nay, I was frequently notified of the passage of a traveller along the highway sixty rods off by the scent of his pipe.

There is commonly sufficient space about us. Our horizon is never quite at our elbows. The thick wood is not just at our door, nor the pond, but somewhat is always clearing, familiar and worn by us, appropriated and fenced in some way, and reclaimed from Nature. For what reason have I this vast range and circuit, some square miles of unfrequented forest, for my privacy, abandoned to me by men? My nearest neighbor is a mile distant, and no house is visible from any place but the hill-tops within half a mile of my own. I have my horizon bounded by woods all to myself; a distant view of the railroad where it touches the pond on the one hand, and of the fence which skirts the woodland road on the other. But for the most part it is as solitary where I live as on the prairies. It is as much Asia or Africa as New England. I have, as it were, my own sun and moon and stars, and a little world all to myself. At night there was never a traveller passed my house, or knocked at my door, more than if I were the first or last man; unless it were in the spring, when at long intervals some came from the village to fish for pouts — they plainly fished much more in the Walden Pond of their own natures, and baited their hooks with darkness — but they soon retreated, usually with light baskets, and left "the world to darkness and to me," and the black kernel of the night was never profaned by any human neighborhood. I believe that men are generally still a little afraid of the dark, though the witches are all hung, and Christianity and candles have been introduced.

Yet I experienced sometimes that the most sweet and tender, the most innocent and encouraging society may be found in any natural object, even for the poor misanthrope and most melancholy man. There can be no very black melancholy to him who lives in the midst of Nature and has his senses still. There was never yet such a storm but it was Æolian music[2] to a healthy and innocent ear. Nothing can rightly compel a simple and brave man to a vulgar sadness. While I enjoy the friendship of the seasons I trust that nothing can make life a burden to me. The gentle rain which waters my beans and keeps me in the house today is not drear and melancholy, but good for me too. Though it prevents my hoeing them, it is of far more worth than my hoeing. If it should continue so long as to cause the seeds to rot in the ground and destroy the potatoes in the low lands, it would still be good for the grass on the uplands, and, being good for the grass, it would be good for me. Sometimes, when I compare myself with other men, it seems as if I were more favored by the gods than they, beyond any deserts that I am conscious of; as if I had a warrant and surety at their hands which my fellows have not, and were especially guided and guarded. I do not flatter myself, but if it be possible they flatter me. I have never felt lonesome, or in the least oppressed by a sense of solitude, but once, and that was a few weeks after I came to the woods, when, for an hour, I doubted if the near neighborhood of man was not essential to a serene and healthy life. To be alone was something unpleasant. But I was at the same time conscious of a slight insanity in my mood, and seemed to foresee my recovery. In the midst of a gentle rain while these thoughts prevailed, I was suddenly sensible of such sweet and beneficent society in Nature, in the very pattering of the drops, and in every sound and sight around my house, an infinite and unaccountable friendliness all at once

---

2) Æolian music: 그리스 신화에서 이올로스는 바람의 신으로 고대 그리스 사람들은 바람이 불면 저절로 울리는 악기를 만들어 이를 이올리안 하프라고 불렀다. 여기에서 이올리안 음악이란 바로 숲에 바람이 불어 만들어내는 아름다운 소리를 말함.

like an atmosphere sustaining me, as made the fancied advantages of human neighborhood insignificant, and I have never thought of them since. Every little pine needle expanded and swelled with sympathy and befriended me. I was so distinctly made aware of the presence of something kindred to me, even in scenes which we are accustomed to call wild and dreary, and also that the nearest of blood to me and humanest was not a person nor a villager, that I thought no place could ever be strange to me again.

Some of my pleasantest hours were during the long rain-storms in the spring or fall, which confined me to the house for the afternoon as well as the forenoon, soothed by their ceaseless roar and pelting; when an early twilight ushered in a long evening in which many thoughts had time to take root and unfold themselves. In those driving northeast rains which tried the village houses so, when the maids stood ready with mop and pail in front entries to keep the deluge out, I sat behind my door in my little house, which was all entry, and thoroughly enjoyed its protection. In one heavy thunder-shower the lightning struck a large pitch pine across the pond, making a very conspicuous and perfectly regular spiral groove from top to bottom, an inch or more deep, and four or five inches wide, as you would groove a walking-stick. I passed it again the other day, and was struck with awe on looking up and beholding that mark, now more distinct than ever, where a terrific and resistless bolt came down out of the harmless sky eight years ago. Men frequently say to me, "I should think you would feel lonesome down there, and want to be nearer to folks, rainy and snowy days and nights especially." I am tempted to reply to such—This whole earth which we inhabit is but a point in space. How far apart, think you, dwell the two most distant inhabitants of yonder star, the breadth of whose disk cannot be appreciated by our instruments? Why should I feel lonely? is not our planet in the Milky Way? This which you put seems to me not to be the most important question. What sort of space is that which separates a man from his fellows and makes him solitary? I have found that no exertion of the legs can bring two minds much nearer to one another[3]. What do we want most to dwell near to? Not to many men surely, the depot, the post-office, the bar-room, the meeting-house, the school-house, the grocery, Beacon Hill[4], or the Five Points[5], where men most congregate, but to the perennial source of our life, whence in all our experience we have found that to issue, as the willow stands near the water and sends out its roots in that direction. This will vary with different natures, but this is the place where a wise man will dig his cellar……. I one evening overtook one of my townsmen, who has accumulated what is called "a handsome property"—though I never got a *fair* view of it—on the Walden road, driving a pair of cattle to market, who inquired of me how I could bring my mind to give up so many of the comforts of

3) I have found that no exertion of the legs can bring two minds much nearer to one another: being physically closer to someone does not mean you understand each other's minds or are mentally closer.

4) Beacon Hill : fashionable section of Boston

5) the Five Points: former disreputable section of New York City, between the current New York City Hall and Chinatown

life. I answered that I was very sure I liked it passably well; I was not joking. And so I went home to my bed, and left him to pick his way through the darkness and the mud to Brighton — or Bright-town — which place he would reach some time in the morning.

Any prospect of awakening or coming to life to a dead man makes indifferent all times and places. The place where that may occur is always the same, and indescribably pleasant to all our senses. For the most part we allow only outlying and transient circumstances to make our occasions. They are, in fact, the cause of our distraction. Nearest to all things is that power which fashions their being. *Next* to us the grandest laws are continually being executed. *Next* to us is not the workman whom we have hired, with whom we love so well to talk, but the workman whose work we are.

"How vast and profound is the influence of the subtile powers of Heaven and of Earth!"

"We seek to perceive them, and we do not see them; we seek to hear them, and we do not hear them; identified with the substance of things, they cannot be separated from them."

"They cause that in all the universe men purify and sanctify their hearts, and clothe themselves in their holiday garments to offer sacrifices and oblations to their ancestors. It is an ocean of subtile intelligences. They are everywhere, above us, on our left, on our right; they environ us on all sides[6]."

We are the subjects of an experiment which is not a little interesting to me. Can we not do without the society of our gossips a little while under these circumstances—have our own thoughts to cheer us? Confucius says truly, "Virtue does not remain as an abandoned orphan; it must of necessity have neighbors[7]."

With thinking we may be beside ourselves in a sane sense. By a conscious effort of the mind we can stand aloof from actions and their consequences; and all things, good and bad, go by us like a torrent. We are not wholly involved in Nature. I may be either the driftwood in the stream, or Indra[8] in the sky looking down on it. I *may* be affected by a theatrical exhibition; on the other hand, I *may not* be affected by an actual event which appears to concern me much more. I only know myself as a human entity; the scene, so to speak, of thoughts and affections; and am sensible of a certain doubleness by which I can stand as remote from myself as from another. However intense my experience, I am conscious of the presence and criticism of a part of me, which, as it were, is not a part of me, but spectator, sharing no experience, but taking note of it, and that is no more I than it is you. When the play, it may be the tragedy, of life is over, the spectator goes his way. It was a kind of fiction, a work of the imagination only, so far as he was concerned. This doubleness may easily make us poor neighbors and friends sometimes.

I find it wholesome to be alone the greater part of the time. To be in

---

6) 위의 세 인용문은 공자의 『중용』에서 나온 것.

7) 『논어』 참조.

8) Indra: in Hinduism, chief of the Vedic gods, god of thunder, & rain

company, even with the best, is soon wearisome and dissipating. I love to be alone. I never found the companion that was so companionable as solitude. We are for the most part more lonely when we go abroad among men than when we stay in our chambers. A man thinking or working is always alone, let him be where he will. Solitude is not measured by the miles of space that intervene between a man and his fellows. The really diligent student in one of the crowded hives of Cambridge College is as solitary as a dervish in the desert. The farmer can work alone in the field or the woods all day, hoeing or chopping, and not feel lonesome, because he is employed; but when he comes home at night he cannot sit down in a room alone, at the mercy of his thoughts, but must be where he can "see the folks[9]," and recreate, and as he thinks remunerate himself for his day's solitude; and hence he wonders how the student can sit alone in the house all night and most of the day without ennui and "the blues[10]"; but he does not realize that the student, though in the house, is still at work in *his* field, and chopping in *his* woods, as the farmer in his, and in turn seeks the same recreation and society that the latter does, though it may be a more condensed form of it.

Society is commonly too cheap. We meet at very short intervals, not having had time to acquire any new value for each other. We meet at meals three times a day, and give each other a new taste of that old musty

9) "see the folks": see his family

10) "the blues": melancholy, sadness

cheese that we are. We have had to agree on a certain set of rules, called etiquette and politeness, to make this frequent meeting tolerable and that we need not come to open war. We meet at the post-office, and at the sociable, and about the fireside every night; we live thick and are in each other's way, and stumble over one another, and I think that we thus lose some respect for one another. Certainly less frequency would suffice for all important and hearty communications. Consider the girls in a factory —never alone, hardly in their dreams. It would be better if there were but one inhabitant to a square mile, as where I live. The value of a man is not in his skin, that we should touch him.

I have heard of a man lost in the woods and dying of famine and exhaustion at the foot of a tree, whose loneliness was relieved by the grotesque visions with which, owing to bodily weakness, his diseased imagination surrounded him, and which he believed to be real. So also, owing to bodily and mental health and strength, we may be continually cheered by a like but more normal and natural society, and come to know that we are never alone.

I have a great deal of company in my house; especially in the morning, when nobody calls. Let me suggest a few comparisons, that some one may convey an idea of my situation. I am no more lonely than the loon in the pond that laughs so loud, or than Walden Pond[11] itself. What company

11) Walden Pond: 1845년부터 약 2년간 Thoreau가 오두막집을 짓고 살았던 미국 메사추세츠 Walden 숲에 있는 호수.

has that lonely lake, I pray? And yet it has not the blue devils, but the blue angels in it, in the azure tint of its waters. The sun is alone, except in thick weather, when there sometimes appear to be two, but one is a mock sun. God is alone — but the devil, he is far from being alone; he sees a great deal of company; he is legion. I am no more lonely than a single mullein or dandelion in a pasture, or a bean leaf, or sorrel, or a horse-fly, or a bumblebee. I am no more lonely than the Mill Brook, or a weathercock, or the north star, or the south wind, or an April shower, or a January thaw, or the first spider in a new house.

I have occasional visits in the long winter evenings, when the snow falls fast and the wind howls in the wood, from an old settler and original proprietor, who is reported to have dug Walden Pond, and stoned it, and fringed it with pine woods; who tells me stories of old time and of new eternity; and between us we manage to pass a cheerful evening with social mirth and pleasant views of things, even without apples or cider — a most wise and humorous friend, whom I love much, who keeps himself more secret than ever did Goffe or Whalley[12]; and though he is thought to be dead, none can show where he is buried. An elderly dame, too, dwells in my neighborhood, invisible to most persons, in whose odorous herb garden I love to stroll sometimes, gathering simples and listening to her fables; for she has a genius of unequalled fertility, and her memory runs back far-

12) Goffe or Whalley: William Goffe, Edward Whalley, indicted for killing Charles I of England, lived in hiding in America

ther than mythology, and she can tell me the original of every fable, and on what fact every one is founded, for the incidents occurred when she was young. A ruddy and lusty old dame, who delights in all weathers and seasons, and is likely to outlive all her children yet.

The indescribable innocence and beneficence of Nature — of sun and wind and rain, of summer and winter — such health, such cheer, they afford forever! and such sympathy have they ever with our race, that all Nature would be affected, and the sun's brightness fade, and the winds would sigh humanely, and the clouds rain tears, and the woods shed their leaves and put on mourning in midsummer, if any man should ever for a just cause grieve. Shall I not have intelligence with the earth? Am I not partly leaves and vegetable mould myself?

Wine Basics: Grape Varieties

Wines are made from hundreds of different grape varieties[1], each one imparting specific characteristics. In some regions, one grape variety is used to make a wine; in others, winemakers blend several varieties in a single wine. Here are a dozen of the world's best and most widely used grape varieties. For each one, I will discuss what wine people call "varietal character," or the special qualities of the grape.

A. White Wine Grapes

Chardonnay. The hottest[2] grape for white wines among American wine

1) varieties: 종류, 품종
2) the hottest: 가장 인기 있는, 가장 잘 팔리는

aficionados[3], Chardonnay is low in varietal character—that is, the grape itself does not have immediately recognizable, identifiable flavors. It ripens well, meaning that the wine can be rich, a little sweet, high in alcohol—all things that the American wine-buying public seems to like. It takes beautifully to[4] a range of barrel techniques, such as fermentation in the barrels and the stirring up of yeast, which ultimately give the wine flavors not derived from the grape itself. So when you open a Chardonnay, you may smell and taste tropical fruit (pineapple often appears), bubble gum, toast, vanilla or spice (such as clove). My favorite Chardonnay flavors are earthy-minerally, often derived from the chalky soil of Burgundy (especially Chablis, a French village in Northern Burgundy that turns out spectacular Chardonnay-based wines). A great white Burgundy (which is made from the Chardonnay grape) grown in a top vineyard and made by a master winemaker can be a complex delight when aged for ten years or so[5].

Sauvignon Blanc. This grape is easy to identify in a blind tasting. What's hard is finding the words to describe it. When Sauvignon Blanc is grown in a cool area, the resulting wine is herbal, even vegetal—some of the world's Sauvignon Blancs suggest canned asparagus. Sometimes a quality creeps in—trust me, this is attractive—that is reminiscent of swea-

3) aficionados: [Sp.] 열렬한 애호가들
4) take beautifully to: ~에 아주 훌륭하게 들어맞다[적응하다]
5) when aged for ten years or so: 10년 이상 숙성되었을 때

ty clothes left in a gym locker. Winemakers often try to eliminate the varietal character of Sauvignon Blanc, which not everyone likes, by letting the grapes get very ripe, which gives the wine more general fruit qualities. Too bad. These days, even Sancerre (France's classic wine made from Sauvignon Blanc grapes) often doesn't taste "green" enough. The gap is being filled by Sauvignon Blancs from New Zealand, and some good ones from South Africa.

Riesling. In the 19th century, Riesling — not Chardonnay — was commonly considered the world's greatest white wine grape variety. Why? Because it's capable of making wine that really has "breed," as wine writers like to say, also described as "elegance" and "refinement." It doesn't taste hot, fat, flabby or "out of control" in any way. When Riesling is good, it combines a whole range of fruit flavors with a steely acidity that keeps the wine taut, which means crisp and low in alcohol. Young Riesling wines can smell like peaches, mint, lime, honey; as they age, they begin taking on desirable "petrol," or gasoline-like, tones. To Riesling freaks[6)], the appearance of these minerally scents is cause for celebration. You may have heard that all Riesling wine is sweet. Not so: Much of the Riesling made in Germany and Austria is actually dry[7)]. In addition, some of the world's greatest dessert wines (such as Germany's Eiswein and

---

6) freaks: 열광자들, 광(狂)들

7) dry: (포도주 등의) 맛이 산뜻한, 톡 쏘는, 달콤한 종류가 아닌(opp. sweet)

Trockenbeerenauslese) also can be made from Riesling.

Gewurztraminer. The one grape that most wine-lovers would immediately flag in a blind tasting is Gewurztraminer, because its aromas and tastes are so distinctive. Unfortunately, describing it is not as easy as identifying it. Most wine people know that "wurz" means "spice," and therefore blithely describe the varietal character of Gewurztraminer as "spicy." But it doesn't really smell like any spice I know. The most powerful olfactory[8)] reference, for me, is fresh lychee fruit. Many proclaim that Gewurztraminer is the perfect wine for spicy food. But beware — Gewurz can be bitter and high in alcohol — two qualities that don't play well at all with food that's "hot" with spices. To make things even trickier, most Gewurztraminer produced in Alsace, the home of the world's best Gewurz, is dry, but not all of it is so. In California, on the other hand, most of it is lightly sweet. Bottom line: Be really careful when matching Gewurz with food. It's an exciting stand-alone wine, but not a high-odds proposition at table.

Trebbiano. This grape is included by dint of its ubiquity[9)]: It is the Italian grape for white wine. It is planted all over the Italian peninsula, and is used for everything from Soave, the famous white wine of the

8) olfactory: 후각의, 후관(嗅官)의
9) ubiquity: 도처에 있음, 편재(遍在)

Veneto region, to balsamic vinegar. Is it good? Not particularly — especially if you're looking for great varietal character in your white wine. It is, however, pleasant and serviceable. Trebbiano can create crisp, clean, light wines that are terrific partners for all kinds of Italian dishes. One of my favorite wines from Trebbiano is a super-light, highly refreshing Tuscan white called Galestro, which gets no respect in the U.S. but is guzzled by the ton[10] in Italy.

Pinot Gris. Most Italian wines from this grape variety have the Italian version of the name, Pinot Grigio, right on the label. As it's made in Italy, however, Pinot Grigio (or Pinot Gris) doesn't have a great deal of varietal character. Move over to France, on the other hand, and you can see why wine-lovers sometimes rave about Pinot Gris. In the vineyards of Alsace in northeastern France, Pinot Gris is a different creature altogether. It's a much heavier, riper, more explosive wine, with some of that high-octane melon and spice that belongs to Alsace alone. This wine is not particularly flexible with food, but it is wonderful for a cold terrine of foie gras — a match served thousands of times a day in Alsace.

10) guzzled by the ton: 엄청나게 마셔대는

B. Red Wine Grapes

Cabernet Sauvignon. If Chardonnay is the vanilla of today's commercial climate, Cabernet Sauvignon is the chocolate. These two "flavors" dominate wine lists and wine shops in America. Historically, Cabernet Sauvignon is the major grape variety used in the great wines of Bordeaux's Medoc region in western France, and all the textbooks say that these wines are the world's greatest reds[11]. Cabernet Sauvignon is easy to pick out in a blind tasting—the varietal character, like that of the white Sauvignon grape, has to do with herbs and vegetables (bell pepper is a favorite taster's image). But great Cabernet goes beyond that; in youth, it often includes divine whiffs of red fruits, such as raspberry. As it ages, good Cabernet Sauvignon gets even more interesting, picking up a whole spectrum of aromas[12] — of which cedar, or "cigar box," is the most classic. Because top-quality, expensive Cabernet Sauvignon can be fiercely tannic in youth, it often needs 15 to 20 years to shed its tannins, develop deep flavor and reach its best.

Merlot. Merlot is another grape in the classic Bordeaux blend. Because the textbooks say Merlot is used to "soften" Cabernet, a myth spread: Merlot is the soft one, round and gentle, not tannic. It is true that if you

11) reds: red wines

12) a whole spectrum of aromas: 가지각색의 향, 온갖 향

grow Merlot a certain way in certain places, it will fit that profile. But you can grow soft Cabernet, too, and you can grow a tough Merlot. In fact, Merlot's varietal character is not far from that of Cabernet Sauvignon; it's easy to mix them up in a blind tasting. The tell-tale Merlot quality— look for it in wines named for the French Pomerol and Saint-Emilion regions—is a scent reminiscent of the floor of a pine forest with lots of fallen needles. Merlot, too, can be fruity, even jammy, in youth, and then can age into something complex, mysterious and magnificent.

Pinot Noir. Unlike the Bordeaux region, Burgundy, in eastern France, usually makes red wine from one grape alone, and that grape is the incomparable Pinot Noir. Pinot is more delicate and subtle than Cabernet Sauvignon or Merlot. In youth, the emphasis is on strawberry-like and cherry-like red fruit (not on herbal qualities as in Cabernet); experienced Pinot-spotters sometimes look for a whiff of geranium as a Pinot clue. In youth, Pinot—though it can be tannic—is rarely as austere as Cabernet; much Pinot Noir gives pleasure after two or three years of aging, while many Cabernets need many more years to be palatable[13]. When a great Pinot Noir that is meant to age reaches its climax—the best ones can easily go 15 or 20 years—you have one of the most extraordinary experiences in all of wine. Some hints of cherries and strawberries may remain, alongside the orgasmic array of earthy, animal-like, erotic, truffly aromas that

13) palatable: 맛 좋은, 입에 맞는

defy description[14] (and would defy a censor).

Syrah. One of the greats of southeastern France's Rhone Valley, Syrah is a grape with power and weight. Syrah is the backbone of such thick wines as those from the French appellations of Cote Rotie, Cornas and Hermitage. Often quite dark and purple in youth, textbooks call it "peppery," as in freshly ground black pepper, but I find it more animal-like, or "sauvage," as the French like to say, meaning "wild," actually smelling like wild animals. A nice feature of Syrah is that less expensive examples of it, such as those from St. Joseph or Crozes-Hermitage, can have complexity and give pleasure after only three or four years in the bottle. The really great Syrahs — such as Hermitage from a great producer in a great year — can evolve for decades into the same kind of indescribable nuance and mystery that old Cabernet Sauvignon or old Pinot Noir can yield. Much Syrah was planted in California in the '90s, and Shiraz — the Australian name for Syrah — is the workhorse red grape of the Australian wine industry.

Zinfandel. Though no one knows exactly where this grape came from — the current belief is that it is a transplant from Puglia, in southern Italy — it is indisputably California's grape today, with almost no winemakers in other places producing it. It's actually made in a variety of styles in

14) defy description: 이루 다 말[묘사]할 수 없는

California, from elegant to brutal. But the quintessential Zin-ness always comes through: Red fruits and berries, but with a wild, zesty, almost minty aroma that's often called "brambly." You simply have to try it to get a sense of its varietal character. Try a bottle not more than three or four years old, because that's when the Zin character is strongest.

Gamay. The grape of southern Burgundy's Beaujolais region is a heck of a lot simpler and less important than the other grapes on this roster[15]. But why hold that against it? When you're drinking wine every day with your meals, "impressive" gets tired fast. The aroma of young Gamay (most Beaujolais is consumed within one or two years of harvest) is unmistakable: A lighthearted wave of cherry-strawberry fruit sweeps over you, sometimes joined by something so sweetly, irrepressibly fruity it smells like ripe banana. On the palate, Gamay wines are bright, reasonably crisp with acid and moderate in alcohol, with little noticeable tannin. In other words: Wines from Gamay grapes are ideal for all kinds of foods. There are a number of grape varieties in California with "Gamay" in their names, but none are the true "Gamay" of France's Beaujolais region.

---

15) roster: 명부, 목록

Dead Poets Society

Directed by Peter Weir

Cast

Robin Williams .... John Keating

Robert Sean Leonard .... Neil Perry

Ethan Hawke .... Todd Anderson

Josh Charles .... Knox Overstreet

Gale Hansen .... Charles Dalton

17 INT. ENGLISH CLASSROOM - DAY

The junior students — Todd, Neil, Knox, Charlie, Cameron, Meeks and some of the others we've seen — enter. They are loaded down with books and look weary. Sitting in the front of the room, staring out the window is JOHN KEATING, the teacher we glimpsed earlier. He wears a collared shirt, tie, no jacket.

The boys take seats and settle in. Keating stares out the window a long time. The students start to shuffle uncomfortably. Finally Keating stands, picks up a yardstick, and begins slowly strolling the aisles.

He stops and stares into the face of one of the boys.

KEATING: (to the blushing boy) Don't be embarrassed. He moves off, then stops in front of Charlie Dalton.

KEATING: (CONT'D) (as if discovering something known only to himself) Uh-huh
(he moves to Todd Anderson) Uh-huh
(he moves to Neil Perry) Ha!

Keating slaps his free hand with the yardstick, then strides to the front of the room.

KEATING: (CONT'D) Nimble young minds!

He steps up onto the desk, turns and faces the class.

KEATING: (CONT'D) (energetically) Oh Captain, My Captain[1]. Who knows where that's from?

No one raises a hand.

KEATING: (CONT'D) It was written by a poet named Walt Whitman about Mr. Abraham Lincoln. In this class you may refer to me as either Mr. Keating, or Oh Captain, My Captain.

Keating steps down and starts. strolling the aisles.

KEATING: (CONT'D) So that I become the source of as few rumors as possible, let me tell you that yes, I was a student at this institution many moons ago[2], and no, at that time I did not possess this charismatic personality. However, should you choose to emulate my manner, it can only help your grade. Pick up a textbook from the back, gentlemen, and let's retire to the honor room.

He steps off the desk and walks out. The students sit, not sure what to do, then realize they are to follow him. They quickly gather their books, pick up texts, and follow.

---

1) "Oh Captain, My Captain" : 미국시인 월트 휘트먼이 자신이 존경했던 링컨 대통령의 죽음을 애도하여 쓴 시.

2) many moons ago: 오래 전에

18 INT. THE WELTON OAK PANELED HONOR ROOM - DAY

This is the room where the boys waited earlier. The walls are lined with class pictures: dating back into the 1800s. School trophies of every description fill trophy cases and shelves. Keating leads the students in, then faces the class.

KEATING: Mister……

(Keating looks at his roll)

Pitts. An unfortunate name. Stand up, Mister Pitts.

Pitts stands.

KEATING: (CONT'D) Open your text, Pitts, to page forty and read for us the first stanza of the poem.

Pitts looks through his book. He finds the poem.

PITTS: To The Virgins to Make Much Of Time?[3)]

KEATING: That's the one.

---

3) "To the Virgins, to Make Much of Time" : 영국시인 Robert Herrick이 쓴, 현세를 즐기라는 내용의 시.

Giggles in the class. Pitts reads.

PITTS: Gather ye rosebuds[4] while ye may
Old time is still a flying
And this same flower that smiles today
Tomorrow will be dying.

KEATING: Gather ye rosebuds while ye may. The Latin term for that sentiment is "Carpe Diem[5]." Anyone know what that means?

MEEKS: Carpe Diem··· seize the day.

KEATING: Very good, Mr._?

MEEKS: Meeks.

KEATING: Seize the day while you're young, see that you make use of your time. Why does the poet write these lines?

A STUDENT:

Because he's in a hurry?

---

4) Gather ye rosebuds: '현재를 즐기라'는 뜻.

5) Carpe Diem: catch the day, seize the present. 현재를 즐기라는 뜻의 라틴어.

KEATING: Because we're food for worms, lads! Because we're only going to experience a limited number of springs, summers, and falls. One day, hard as it is to believe[6], each and every one of us is going to stop breathing, turn cold, and die! Stand up and peruse the faces of the boys who attended this school sixty or seventy years ago. Don't be timid, go look at them.

The boys get up. Todd, Neil, Knox, Meeks, etc. go over to the class pictures that line the honor room walls.

ANGLES ON VARIOUS PICTURES ON THE WALLS.
Faces of young men stare at us from out of the past.

KEATING: They're not that different than any of you, are they? There's hope in their eyes, just like in yours. They believe themselves destined for wonderful things, just like many of you. Well, where are those smiles now, boys? What of that hope?

THE BOYS are staring at the pictures, sobered[7] by what Keating is saying.

KEATING: (CONT'D) Did most of them not wait until it was too late be-

6) hard as it is to believe: 믿기 어렵겠지만
7) sobered: 진지해져, 침착해져, 엄숙해져

fore making their lives into even one iota of what they were capable?
In chasing the almighty deity of success did they not squander their boyhood dreams? Most of those gentlemen are fertilizing daffodils! However, if you get very close, boys, you can hear them whisper. Go ahead, lean in. near it?
(loud whisper)
'Carpe Diem, lads. Seize the day. Make your lives extra-ordinary.'

Todd, Neil, Knox, Charlie, Cameron, Meeks, Pitts all stare into the pictures on the wall. All are lost in thought.

19 EXT. THE WELTON CAMPUS - DAY

The class files out of the honor room. Todd, Neil, Knox, Charlie, Cameron, Necks, and Pitts walk together, books in hand. All thinking about what just happened in class.

PITTS: Weird.

NEIL: But different.

KNOX: Spooky if you ask me.

CAMERON: You think he'll test us on that stuff?

CHARLIE: Oh come on, Cameron, don't you get anything?

English Readings

2007년 3월 10일 초판 발행
2010년 2월 25일 재판 1쇄 발행
2011년 8월 15일 재판 2쇄 발행

지은이 이혜경, 안필규, 이 철
펴낸이 이찬규
펴낸곳 북코리아
등 록 제03-01240호
주 소 462-807 경기도 성남시 중원구 상대원동 146-8
우림2차 A동 1007호
전 화 02-704-7840
팩 스 02-704-7848
이메일 sunhaksa@korea.com
홈페이지 www.bookorea.co.kr

값 11,000원

ISBN 978-89-92521-14-7 (93740)